"Ministry is hard work. I appreciate th... experience. She practically breaks down how to help you develop systems. Whether you're beginning in ministry or on the brink of quitting, this book is a great reminder that it's not about doing ministry alone, but about you and your church thriving as you develop the foundational structure for a fruitful and lasting ministry."

Yancy, songwriter and worship leader for kids and families, Yancy Ministries, Inc.

"If you are looking for a book to help you be incredibly strategic with life-changing results in children's ministry, then this book is for you. Think of Mark and Annette as your personal leaders and consultants to help take your ministry to the next level. I love both the strategy and the practicality."

Jim Burns, president of HomeWord, author of *Understanding Your Teen* and *The First Few Years of Marriage*

"Wow! This book is awesome. Finally, we have the definitive children's ministry book. With personal experiences that are all too familiar for those of us in ministry, Mark DeVries and Annette Safstrom provide practical ideas for building solid, impactful opportunities for children and their families. *Sustainable Children's Ministry* has encouraged and excited me about the future of my ministry!"

Kathy McCarron, director of children and family ministries, NorthPark Presbyterian Church, Dallas

"There's hope for every tired and frustrated children's ministry worker out there, and you'll find it in this book. It's a step-by-step guide to building a healthy, effective, and collaborative children's ministry, and how to actually enjoy your ministry job again. Don't walk—run to read this book!"

Mary Beth Abplanalp, youth minister

"It has been many years since I received that frantic call from my pastor saying that the previous children's pastor just resigned and he thought I'd be perfect for the job. I've learned a lot in the intervening years of ministry. And some of that learning came from the work of Mark DeVries. Now, with the partnership of an experienced children's pastor, Annette Safstrom, Mark has finally moved into my neighborhood of children's ministry. As I read this systematic and well-organized book, I wished that I'd had such an easy-to-follow plan all those years ago. It would have saved my sanity over and over again!"

Trevecca Okholm, adjunct professor of practical theology, Azusa Pacific University, author of *Kingdom Family: Re-Envisioning God's Plan for Marriage and Family*

"People who like cooking love the idea of a box that contains pre-portioned food and cooking instructions. *Sustainable Children's Ministry* is a box with ingredients that offer what it takes to construct and maintain a healthy, well-balanced ministry to kids and family. It comes with a manual written by two people, Annette Safstrom and Mark DeVries, who know the frontlines well. This is the box you get to keep, and it gives you what you need to build a strong ministry and go forward."

Doug Ranck, associate pastor of youth, children, and families, Free Methodist Church, Santa Barbara, CA

"*Sustainable Children's Ministry* gave me a great boost of energy for my work during a time when I greatly needed it. I found myself laughing out loud when I recognized myself in many of the author's own stories including grand mistakes, laments of isolation, and being stymied by the disease of chronic volunteer deficiency. But I also found hope in the very practical approach of encouraging me to be intentional about goals for Christian formation, building systems, using tools, partnering with parents, and clarifying roles."

Laura H. Jernigan, associate pastor of Northwest Presbyterian Church, Atlanta

"Mark DeVries and Annette Safstrom have created an amazing resource for churches and their children's ministries. It's not just a collection of good ideas, but a whole systematic approach to enable your ministry to flourish. DeVries and Safstrom focus on building a culture of shared ministry so that children's ministry workers do not experience frustration and burnout. *Sustainable Children's Ministry* is encouraging, inspiring, practical, and an essential addition to any ministry library."

Lyndsay Lee Slocum, senior associate pastor, Roswell Presbyterian Church

"Annette and Mark have given the church a much-needed gift. It's a valuable guide for children's directors and pastors of churches who want to faithfully reach the next generation. Annette understands the demands and common challenges facing dedicated children's leaders. In a winsome and vulnerable style, she provides coaching in how to develop strong organizational systems and processes, and personal practices that build a sustainable and joyful ministry. The book is compelling and immensely helpful, and is full of practical tools and a good dose of humor!"

Kay Broweleit, retired children's and family ministries pastor, Presbyterian Church USA

"If your hope to help children and parents know that the God of the universe loves them and that they can know, love, and serve this God in return, yet you find yourself frantically busy and overwhelmed, authors Mark DeVries and Annette Safstrom would diagnose you with chronic volunteer deficiency. Easy-to-implement remedies are available on every page of their new book *Sustainable Children's Ministry*. I cannot agree more that 'putting functional systems in place will never be urgent, but without them, everything becomes urgent.' This book just may transform your children's ministry and restore a sense of joy and purpose to your whole church."

Kendy Easley, executive pastor, Bethany Community Church, Seattle

"This is the book I wish I had had twenty years ago when I first started in children's ministry. I knew I wanted to do things differently but was not quite sure how. This is also the book I need to remind me to tend to the systems and not get bogged down putting out fires. The work of the church should continue well beyond any one person or leader, and *Sustainable Children's Ministry* helps the people of God, whether paid or not, to live and serve in the ways God has gifted and called them."

Holly Dittrich, executive pastor, First United Methodist Church, Hurst, TX

"If you need wise friends to walk you through developing a meaningful children's ministry built around systems that make sense and minimize chaos, take the time to read this book. Full of good advice, real-life examples, and strategies for remaining joyful while serving the church, Annette's and Mark's words are manna for people who want to do this work well for a long time."

Elizabeth Cole Goodrich, associate pastor for discipleship,
Independent Presbyterian Church, Birmingham, AL

"In a ministry culture where gimmicks and entertainment can overshadow the reason we serve, it is refreshing to read a book that keeps the essentials and the eternal front and center. Whether you are new to ministry or a seasoned pro, *Sustainable Children's Ministry* is for you. Proven, practical steps mixed with just enough real-life ministry examples provide the reader with a resource to build a ministry from scratch, evaluate an existing ministry, or tweak a program to make it strong until the end."

Danielle Bell, minister to children, Dawson Family of Faith, Birmingham, AL

"Children's ministries need this book! It is packed full of practical and proven training that will help you get out of the weekly whirlwind and focus on what matters most. A must-read for anyone ministering to children and families."
Zach Coffin, director of next generation discipleship for the Wesleyan Church

"This book is a game-changer for the world of children's ministry. It accurately identifies the pitfalls and the challenges that most ministry leaders encounter and responds with practical, systematic methods to implement. I highly recommend this book to anyone in children's ministry as a roadmap to create a thriving, healthy ministry environment that brings out the best in your leadership."
Gina McClain, global children's pastor, Faith Promise Church, Knoxville, TN

"As a children's pastor, this is a must-read. *Sustainable Children's Ministry* will be my go-to guide for many years to come because I have seen the elements of this book transform our church's ministry to children and families in just a few years. DeVries and Safstrom speak to the specific struggles of children's ministry and show how to practically lead from a place of chaos into order."
Casey Cramer, pastor of children, youth, and families, Christ Presbyterian Church, Nashville

"Leading has always mattered when it comes to ministry, and with today's multifaceted pace, strategy matters as well. *Sustainable Children's Ministry* offers a soup-to-nuts approach for building a sure foundation upon which children, volunteers, parents, and those in charge can be cultivated. I look forward to watching this book lead to continued evolution in congregational children's ministry in the months and years to come."
Kris Bjorke, cofounder and director of InterServe Ministries

sustainable children's ministry

from last-minute scrambling to long-term solutions

Mark DeVries and Annette Safstrom

IVP Books

An imprint of InterVarsity Press
Downers Grove, Illinois

InterVarsity Press
P.O. Box 1400, Downers Grove, IL 60515-1426
ivpress.com
email@ivpress.com

InterVarsity Press® is the book-publishing division of InterVarsity Christian Fellowship/USA®, a movement of students and faculty active on campus at hundreds of universities, colleges, and schools of nursing in the United States of America, and a member movement of the International Fellowship of Evangelical Students. For information about local and regional activities, visit intervarsity.org.

While any stories in this book are true, some names and identifying information may have been changed to protect the privacy of individuals.

Cover design: Jeff Miller/Faceout Studio
Interior design: Jeanna Wiggins

ISBN 978-0-8308-4522-4 (print)
ISBN 978-0-8308-8847-4 (digital)

Printed in the United States of America ⊖

InterVarsity Press is committed to ecological stewardship and to the conservation of natural resources in all our operations. This book was printed using sustainably sourced paper.

Library of Congress Cataloging-in-Publication Data
Names: DeVries, Mark, author.
Title: Sustainable children's ministry : from last-minute scrambling to long-term solutions / Mark DeVries and Annette Safstrom.
Description: Downers Grove : InterVarsity Press, 2017. | Includes bibliographical references.
Identifiers: LCCN 2017052103 (print) | LCCN 2017052901 (ebook) | ISBN 9780830888474 (eBook) | ISBN 9780830845224 (pbk. : alk. paper)
Subjects: LCSH: Church work with children.
Classification: LCC BV639.C4 (ebook) | LCC BV639.C4 D48 2017 (print) | DDC 259/.22—dc23
LC record available at https://lccn.loc.gov/2017052103

P	21	20	19	18	17	16	15	14	13	12	11	10	9	8	7	6	5	4	3
Y	34	33	32	31	30	29	28	27	26	25	24	23	22	21	20	19			

To those who have made
it their mission to introduce
children to Jesus and his love.
We can't imagine how great
your reward will be!

Contents

Introduction

Mark DeVries

> *Confusion always precedes learning.* . . .
> *Life's grand prizes are guarded by confusion.* . . . *And*
> *really, isn't it true that right before we know the*
> *answer we always don't know the answer.*
>
> ANDY ANDREWS, *THE NOTICER RETURNS*

> *Everyone then who hears these words of mine and acts on*
> *them will be like a wise man who built his house on rock.*
>
> MATTHEW 7:24 (NRSV)

We were finishing up our last visit to historic Midtown Church. It had been an incredible eighteen-month journey. The youth ministry had gone through an undeniable transformation—the youth pastor now felt empowered, a full volunteer team was working together with a well-defined vision and goals, and the culture had shifted from chronic negativity to unbridled enthusiasm.

We were sad this would be our last visit. Then Pastor Janet asked an odd question, "Can you do this same thing for our children's ministry?"

I paused, uncertain. I knew next to nothing about children's ministry, and I was pretty sure the rest of our Youth Ministry Architects team was in the very same boat.

She saw my uncertainty and spoke before I could:

"Listen, it's not really the children's-ministry-specific work that we need help with. We don't need help with crafts or VBS or getting toys for the nursery. Those are things we have down. What our children's ministry needs help with—and desperately—is things such as building volunteers; developing a check-in and follow-up process; creating a parent ministry; designing a great communication plan; finding ways to invite more young families into our church; establishing a clear vision, direction, goals, and structure—that kind of thing. Isn't that what you do?"

I was still pausing. At that point Youth Ministry Architects was still a young ministry. We had worked with less than one hundred churches, helping them build sustainable youth ministries. Youth ministry was the world I knew and understood.

For my entire adult life, thirty-six years of it anyway, youth ministry had been my focus. Some would even argue—I would be one of them—that my first church hired me to do youth ministry *way* before I was an adult myself. (Some of you who have had the privilege of working alongside a youth minister like me may know *exactly* what I'm talking about!)

Finally, I answered, "You know we know next to nothing about children's ministry?"

"Right."

"And you still want us to work with your children's ministry?"

"Right." She was smiling.

And so on the unassailable strength of Pastor Janet's smile, Children's Ministry Architects was born.

Our staff understood how to build sustainable ministry systems. But we also knew that we had to have someone with children's ministry expertise to join our team, and quickly. Little did we know of an entirely separate story going on in Texas.

Enter Annette

Annette Safstrom was two years into building a children's ministry at a new campus of a multisite church in Texas. Unbeknownst to her, the leadership of her church had brought in a group of consultants to secretly observe and evaluate the church's ministries on a Sunday morning.

I'll spare you the details, but suffice it to say that Annette was devastated by the report she received. Despite having well-trained teachers in place ready to welcome children right on time, despite having a game plan in each classroom that created a warm and exciting experience for children, despite the fact that children were having the time of their lives, the report identified a few unexpected issues.

There was a first-time visitor child who used foul language in one of the classrooms; the interim check-in station was in an awkward location; and the new building lacked the kind of "flash" and "pop" that more innovative churches might have for indoor play. They didn't have the same exciting toys, slides, or décor that families in that suburban area had come to expect from newer churches. So in addition to getting to work addressing some of the challenges raised by the evaluation, Annette got curious. So she did what curious people do. She turned to Google.

She googled "church consultants," not even knowing a week before that such a thing existed. She said, "I ran across all kinds of websites—almost all of them featuring well-educated, stuffy looking, old, white men—until I found Youth Ministry Architects."

On the Youth Ministry Architects site, she found a copy of my book, *Sustainable Youth Ministry*. Being a stuffy-looking old man myself, what a relief that she saw the book before my picture! Annette downloaded *Sustainable Youth Ministry* that night and read the whole thing in two days.

Later she told me, somewhat embarrassed, that she cried through much of the book. Having felt the pressure in previous churches to focus on flash over substance, she felt like the book had put words to the longing she had to build a ministry that didn't depend on expensive gimmicks to do faithful children's ministry.

Within a few years, we had more churches asking for help with their children's ministries than we could have ever imagined. And Annette was leading the charge.

Then one day, when Annette and I were working on a project together, she got a mischievous look on her face and said, somewhat unflatteringly, "You know, *Sustainable Youth Ministry* is good and all, but . . ."

She made it clear that some of the principles in *Sustainable Youth Ministry* don't transfer naturally to children's ministry. For example, she said, children's ministry does not tend to attract the stereotypical "superstar" or pied piper like youth ministry does. In chapter two, we'll introduce you to a much more accurate metaphor for the unfortunate role that many *children's* ministry leaders fall into.

Before our conversation was over, we agreed that *Sustainable Children's Ministry* needed to be written and that we should write it together.

Here, in this introduction, is the only place in the book where you'll hear my voice directly. Once you turn the page to chapter one, you'll be reading Annette's voice. Though we both have worked (repeatedly!) on every page of the book, we wanted to put *Sustainable Children's Ministry* in the voice of the one of us who actually lives and breathes children's ministry every day.

About the Book You're Holding

Though the principles outlined in this book will set you up as a children's ministry leader to be much more creative in your ministry than you've ever been, this is not a book of creative ideas to bring more flash and pop to your ministry. If you are in need a book of clever crafts or cutting-edge ideas, there are lots of them out there, but this is not that book.

If you are looking to build a foundation for your ministry that will be standing long after you are gone, you won't be disappointed. Flash and fizz are fun and can be very effective at attracting young families, at least one time. But without sustainable systems beneath the unforgettable moments, the impact is almost always short-lived.

Archimedes, the Greek mathematician and philosopher, said in the third century BC, "Give me a place to stand, and with a lever I will move the whole world."

Sustainable Children's Ministry offers you that "place to stand" and shows you the levers you'll need to get things moving, to create change that you might never have thought possible before in your particular context. It's a book written primarily for the children's ministry professional, whether part-time, full-time, or volunteer. It's also written for senior leadership and the volunteer teams taking responsibility for their church's ongoing ministry to children, birth through fifth or sixth grade.

Annette will introduce you to a number of ministry tools that can, like levers, multiply what you are able to do on your own. Annette offers the picture of trying to pull out a nail with our bare hands instead of using the claw of a hammer. It's an apt depiction of how often children's ministry workers burn themselves out, not for a lack of effort but for a lack of the appropriate tools.

We realize that these ministry tools are not and will never be the reason we do what we do. You can certainly invite kids to experience the love of Jesus without using these tools, but they hold the potential to vastly expand your impact (without vastly expanding the amount of effort required).

When every kid who attends your fall festival has an opportunity to connect with a leader by name, you expand your capacity to connect more kids to Jesus in a sustainable way. When every volunteer is well-trained and coached, fewer children and families wander away from your ministry. When every visitor feels safe, welcomed, and connected, there's a better chance those children and families will stay around and live into a lifelong love of Christ.

Here's how the book is laid out: In chapters one and two, Annette will take you on a poignant and sometimes entertaining journey through her own early years of ministry, offering the blessings of her mistakes so you don't have to make them.

In chapters three through seven, we introduce you to a systems approach to children's ministry and provide a baseline for what "normal" children's ministry usually costs a church. And we'll lay out the essential systems you'll need to build a sustainable children's ministry in your church.

Chapters eight and nine tackle the most persistent challenge we see children's ministries struggling with: building a thriving volunteer team. Between children's and youth ministries, we've shared this volunteer recruitment system with thousands of leaders. And so far, we've never met a single person who has used the system and not had it work.

In chapters ten and eleven, we'll give you a roadmap for navigating the complex waters of church politics and family ministry.

And in chapter twelve through fourteen, we'll focus on *the* most important tool in your toolbox (hint: you can find that secret in the mirror). It is way too rare for children's ministry workers to tend to their own emotional health, passion for Christ, and passion for ministry. To lead a sustainable children's ministry, this normal will need to change.

The good news is that we've made most of the mistakes for you. Hopefully, learning the principles of this book will keep you from having to make them.

Throughout these pages you'll meet quite a cast of characters—pastors, volunteers, children's ministry professionals, and a few courageous practitioners willing to take the risk of trying out a more sustainable approach to ministry. Ordinarily, to protect the identity of those whose stories we tell, we have adjusted names and details but kept the essence of those stories in tact.

As you read, should you want to talk further with either of us, don't hesitate. You can reach us at mark.devries@ministryarchitects .com and annette.safstrom@ministryarchitects.com.

Let's get started.

From Chaos to Clarity

What's So Different About
Sustainable Children's Ministry?

> *There is always a well-known solution to every*
> *human problem—neat, plausible, and wrong.*
>
> H. L. MENCKEN, "THE DIVINE AFFLATUS"

> *In a rapidly changing world, thriving congregations*
> *are nearly ten times more likely to have changed*
> *themselves than are struggling congregations.*
>
> LOVETT H. WEEMS JR.,
> "FAITH COMMUNITIES TODAY," 2015

When I was eight years old, we started attending a new church. My mom told me I would be going to "children's church" (and that I was going to love it).

There were puppets, skits, and games. My mom was right. I *loved* it. For an eight-year-old, what's not to love about a party? Every. Single. Week. I laughed, made friends, and learned Bible Aerobics. (It was the early '80s!)

But beyond the party, I discovered something else. In children's church I learned to love Jesus and to know that—no matter what—he loved me too. During those years I learned to sing to Jesus at night before I went to bed. I learned that God is real, that he is not just the God of the universe, but *my* God too. In children's church it became normal for me to love God with all of my heart.

When I was ready to age out of children's church, Mrs. Geni, our children's pastor, handed me a piece of paper. She said, "I think you can do this." She could see the curious expression on my face.

"I think you can teach younger kids," she said with a grin.

I was eleven years old.

Over the next week she coached me on delivering a lesson for kids. And that Sunday, I shared that lesson with a dozen or so first through fifth graders. The text was John 17:17 (I still remember it to this day).

Over the next six years, Mrs. Geni spent hours upon hours sharing her love for Jesus and children's ministry with me. I also came to love all the aspects of children's ministry that made kids beg their parents to come to church every week.

When I graduated from high school, I pursued training that would lead to a career in children's ministry. I wrestled with some tough questions in my early adult years, and always found that same Jesus I met in children's church was faithful.

Failure to Launch

I started my first full-time job in children's ministry in 1998. I had just received my master's degree, had been married barely a month, and was fully convinced that my life's work would be in children's ministry. This was my moment.

My new title was Elementary Coordinator. I was stepping into a very large church, replacing the previous elementary coordinator, who was to train me and then be my part-time assistant.

I couldn't have been more excited! I had an endless stream of so many ideas; I felt so ready, so well-equipped for this job.

As Shari, my now assistant, trained me, I realized how *big* this little elementary coordinator job was. As I learned the ins and outs of the job, I was quite sure that if Shari ever truly left me on my own, I would be totally lost in all the disconnected tasks.

There were lessons to read, supply lists to make, volunteers to recruit, calendars to fill, church staff meetings, children's ministry staff meetings, supplies to purchase, visuals to make, thank-you notes to send, and don't even get me started on the clunky check-in system that literally made me sick (more on that later).

I began to dive into my responsibilities. I absolutely loved any chance I had to be with kids and connect them to Jesus. Worshiping with a room full of children was the highlight of every week.

But when Monday rolled around, we almost always had something to discuss in our children's ministry staff meeting. And more often than not, I found myself on the hot seat for something I had said or done.

Those meetings started to get old quickly. I was working sixty-plus hours a week. My new husband was traveling all week and only home on the weekends. I was working all weekend, every weekend, only to feel like a tremendous failure when those staff meetings rolled around. My disconnected list of tasks seemed to grow every week, compounded by an endless parade of last-minute changes to the weekend plan. I knew my pace was simply not sustainable.

At the time, I blamed my bosses for making all the last-minute changes, for not appreciating all I was doing, and for just about everything else in my life that wasn't going as I had planned. No one else seemed to understand how hard this job really was. In just a few months I was transformed from a spunky newlywed to an angry, hurt woman living on the edge of tears most of the time.

Looking back, I realize that I had walked in with many assumptions, expecting the church and children's ministry to have some basic systems already in place (though at the time, I couldn't have told you what those systems even were). This was a large and well-respected ministry. How could so much not be in place?

Little did I know, the church was expecting *me* to develop and implement those very systems. Like most children's ministry leaders, I assumed, without even knowing it, that the ministry would thrive with a reasonable amount of joyful effort. Instead, I realized that a lot beneath the surface was missing, and ministry had begun to suck the life out of me. I found out later that I was not alone. But I'm getting ahead of myself.

During these first few months in ministry, I became known for being incredibly disorganized. Our shared office space (mostly my desk and underneath, behind, and in front of it) looked like an explosion at a toy store. It seemed like balls were dropping left and right.

Somehow, I had managed to complete graduate school while juggling four part-time jobs, but I just couldn't wrap my head around how to get done everything that needed to get done to run a healthy, sustainable children's ministry. My learning curve was steep and bumpy.

The last straw for my boss happened on a busy Sunday with lots of moving pieces. (Are there any other kind?) I had forgotten to print out attendance sheets to check in the over two hundred kids who showed up that morning. When they arrived, I wasn't ready. And the next day, I was in hot water.

It was an easy mistake to make since the office and children's classrooms were in totally different buildings. But on the heels of other details that I had missed, I had earned myself a three-month probation. Too many balls were dropping, and yet I was working sixty to eighty hours a week. I had somehow gotten myself into an impossible job.

The probation was my wake-up call that I had to start thinking differently. I determined to figure this (dis)organization thing out. Over the next three months I became laser focused on learning. And many of the strategies I'll share with you were mined during that tenuous three months.

One of my first discoveries was that this job would never fit neatly into nice little boxes. No matter how large or small your ministry is, the list of skills you'll need might include

* recruiter
* trainer
* child development expert
* camp coordinator
* behavior expert
* curriculum expert
* copy-machine repair person
* children's music expert
* security guard
* budgeter
* graphic designer
* event planner
* game leader
* theologian
* meal planner
* website manager

* facilities designer
* marketing expert
* committee chair
* newsletter editor
* PowerPoint designer
* storage expert
* supervisor
* inventor
* smart shopper
* attendance tracker
* greeter
* storyteller
* family counselor
* database and attendance manager

A Second Chance

I made it through probation without losing my job, but I was still burned out, disillusioned, and just plain sad. Eventually, I quit my position, frankly not even sure if I wanted to go to church anymore.

By God's grace, we ended up staying in the church. We had two beautiful baby boys. Though our new house was thirty-five minutes from the church, we made the drive every week. But when our church planted a new campus just three miles from our house, we jumped at the chance.

Before long, the new pastor asked if I would take on the children's ministry. I quickly told him no! It had been five years since I left my job in children's ministry, and I had no intention of going back. That ship had sailed.

I knew what the job of children's ministry was like, and I had no interest in turning my life upside down again. By now, I had my own active family to consider.

When I got home that Sunday, my stomach was churning. I just couldn't quiet the uneasiness. I mentioned it to my husband, and he said, "Well, you should have told him yes. It's your calling, and you turned it down." I knew that he was right, but my vow was to never put myself in that situation again.

Tears welled up in my eyes. I felt torn. I couldn't stop thinking about how hard I had worked before, and how tired and hurt I was in the end. I remembered how so many of my most faithful volunteers, the ones I called on *every* time I was in a pinch, eventually burned out too. I didn't want be part of something like that ever again. I wanted to make sure that if I were to go back and work for the church, I wouldn't be putting our family at risk.

So with a combination of terror and excitement, I called the pastor and told him I had changed my mind. A few days later, I met with the pastor and other church leaders to discuss the details of the job and the children's ministry. The meeting lasted about five hours! (There's a chance maybe I came to the meeting a little overprepared.)

Since this was a brand new campus, I had a clean slate, and I wanted to set up a solid structure this time, something that could hold together without me scurrying around plugging every hole myself. I wanted to make sure I wasn't walking blindly into the same issues I had faced before.

This time, we began differently. Very differently.

What Was Different

We began by creating the systems that would make it possible to support exponential church growth. Sure, there were times when we were stretched thin and struggled to find enough volunteers, but we also made it our mission to protect our volunteers from undue burden that could lead so easily to burnout.

After three years, I handed off the director's position to Shari. We had worked hard on the parts of the ministry that no one was going to notice. There were times that even the church leadership didn't understand all that was in place behind the scenes or why we had decided not to implement some of the flashy "wow" practices found in other large churches.

Initially, my pride was a little hurt when things got *better* after I left! When people would tell Shari what a great job she was doing (and, of course, she was), she would point to all the hard work we had put into setting up the foundation for ministry. Without those foundational systems, she knew she wouldn't have been able to enjoy the installation of an indoor playground or oversee a two-day fall festival that would rival any small-town fair. And through it all, she had the freedom to see her son play high school football, even on Thursday nights when there were demanding programs going on at church.

A Study in Contrast

My two experiences in children's ministry couldn't have been more different. All my great ideas, combined with a total lack of systems and structures in my first position, left me overworked and overwhelmed. I was actually helping to create a crushing toxicity in the ministry culture.

The second time around, we focused first on the behind-the-scenes parts of the ministry, which most folks didn't even know were needed, and we enjoyed a well-paced, thriving ministry in a joyful, collaborative climate. I've come to see ministry structures as a lot like housework: no one notices it unless it's *not* done. Putting foundational systems in place will never be urgent, but without them, everything becomes urgent.

In talking with hundreds of children's ministry workers around the country, I have discovered that my first ministry experience is all too common. When we first start talking about systems in ministry, most people give us a blank stare. They know about curriculum and supplies, and maybe about newsletters and recruiting volunteers. Most don't realize that they are working frantically because the fundamental structures for ministry are missing altogether.

The Telltale Signs of a Systemless Children's Ministry

In this book we want to introduce you to the key systems that will allow your ministry to thrive no matter what stage you are in. But first I want to introduce you to some of the most common characteristics of systemless children's ministries. See if any of them sound familiar.

1. Suffering from chronic volunteer deficiency (CVD). In 100 percent of the churches I've worked with as either a staff member, volunteer, coach, or consultant, recruiting and sustaining volunteers are some of the most important challenges to overcome. They suffer from what we have come to call chronic volunteer deficiency, which is driven by two common realities:

* Families are busy these days. Fewer and fewer people are showing up to attend Sunday school, much less help out.

* The volunteers we have are doing so much work that they are feeling burned out, and when they finally quit, there will be no one to take their place.

If you're facing CVD, you're not alone. You may be combining classes, leading a class every week yourself, using your own family to fill in, or closing classes because there are not enough leaders to go around.

The good news is that there is a cure for CVD. Dozens of churches have overcome CVD by working an intentional recruiting strategy (a recruiting system), one that is so much more than a bulletin announcement or a desperate pulpit plea. We don't offer an easy, five-minute emergency fix. The recruiting system, like all the systems we'll introduce you to, will take time and sustained effort. But churches who have worked this plan report having as many volunteers as they need.

2. Drowning in drama. I know you didn't get into children's ministry expecting drama to be a part of your everyday life, but the reality is that you can't get around it. Without the right foundational structures, tiny problems can get blown out of proportion and quickly become personal.

Here is a simple example: Let's say the DVD player in your toddler class is on the fritz. You are unaware that your volunteers are going without it for several weeks. Those volunteers begin to assume that you don't care about their little class or even know what it is like to spend an hour and a half with twelve toddlers.

The reality is that you don't yet have a system for learning what equipment is not working. The perception that you don't care becomes reality, and something simple turns into something ugly.

3. Feeling chronically busy and overwhelmed. In children's ministry there will always be busy seasons, with summers being especially challenging. Summers combine regular weekly programming *plus* VBS, camps, and mission projects, all of which happen—oh yeah!—while most of your regular volunteers are on vacation.

When I began my first full-time ministry position, I remember my pastor encouraging me by saying, "Annette, it's just a season." But after the season was over, we rolled into the next overwhelming season without a break. It was no longer a season but a lifestyle. Like a hamster on a wheel of constant activity, what was once energizing and productive crosses the line into a spinning ministry lifestyle that begins to eat away at your soul.

4. Being surrounded by negativity and anxiousness. Systemless children's ministries often find themselves working in a climate of growing negativity and anxiousness. Take a look at your volunteers on a Sunday morning. Do they look stressed? They may be feeling anxiety about their roles. They may not be completely sure when or if they hit the mark, or what they need to accomplish to succeed. They may be scurrying around on Sunday mornings, frantic to get through their lessons.

When we hear things like, "If we just had more money . . ." or "why can't we do it like St. Amazing Church down the street, with a slide for the kids to use to enter their classroom?" negativity and anxiety are not far behind. We can also observe our parents—are they excited or apprehensive when dropping off their kids?

When we ministry leaders are exhausted, *our* anxiety and negativity can accelerate and become contagious. If you hear yourself saying more negative things than positive, it's time to change your script. *We* get to tell the story of our ministry. More often than not, we work hard to get a program launched or an event covered, and then we immediately look ahead to the next thing, without celebrating the successes we had.

An Open Invitation

We want to invite you into a journey of creating a new normal for your children's ministry. These "normals" we've identified just now *can* be changed. And this book is designed to help you do it. Be encouraged. In the pages that follow, you'll find tools to help you build the systems that will bless your church with a healthy, sustainable children's ministry.

The Workhorse Syndrome

Moving Beyond a
Do-It-Yourself Ministry

If you want to go fast, go alone.
If you want to go far, go together.

AFRICAN PROVERB

Any time the majority of the people behave a
particular way the majority of the time, the people are
not the problem. The problem is inherent in the system.
As a leader, you own responsibility for the system.

CHRIS MCCHESNEY, SEAN COVEY, AND JIM HULING,
THE FOUR DISCIPLINES OF EXECUTION

Most children's ministry leaders I know didn't know they were on a path to professional children's ministry until they were already there. Many begin their journey, innocently enough, as volunteers, committed to creating a great church experience for their own children. They see a need and immediately jump in to take care of it. Soon they gain a reputation for getting things done, for taking on the many thankless tasks required of any healthy children's ministry.

And then, when the children's director position becomes vacant, these high-capacity supervolunteers step into the gap, often heroically holding things together. Eventually, someone in the church raises the question, "Why are we looking for a new children's director when we already have you? Have you ever thought of doing this work permanently?"

Sound familiar? An astounding number of the best children's ministry leaders I've met tell a remarkably similar story. In the process of *doing* children's ministry, we hear a call. Something about this work makes our hearts sing. We shake our heads and wonder that the work we would gladly volunteer to do we now get to do as a job!

So far so good. But far too often the next part of the story is not quite as pretty. But it is almost as predictable.

Because very few of us have much in the way of formal training in the work we're doing, we scramble to learn as much as we can—a conference here, a half-read book there, articles, blogs, and lots of conversations with friends. It doesn't take long before, a few years into our professional children's ministry careers, the grind of expanding expectations becomes, well, a grind.

The pressure to draw more young families in the church, combined with the expectation of keeping current programs running *and* adding new programs each year, conspires to eat away at the passion that launched us. We begin to realize that if there is a gap in children's programing, families *will* go elsewhere.

Normal constructive criticism and "concerns" voiced by parents, leaders, and fellow staff members poke holes in our unassailable enthusiasm. Before long, our passion has subtly turned to willingness. Willingness becomes obligation. Obligation turns to chronic exhaustion, until the once-passionate children's ministers find themselves increasingly frustrated, frayed, and defensive. If this journey sounds familiar, you're not alone.

This, of course, is a sad state of affairs. But you know what is even sadder? How many children's ministry workers *stay* in this depressing arrangement for decades! They come to believe that the greatness of the need obligates them to hang in there, even though it's been a long time since anything about this work made their hearts sing.

Sure, a few children's ministry professionals take a direct route, mapping out a clear path for education and training, seeking the shortest point between points A and B. From the outset they choose to be Christian educators or children's pastors. I have met a few of these folks. Even though I was one, I found myself struggling with the same issues of the supervolunteer turned children's minister. But my training didn't prepare me for the day-to-day reality of running a children's ministry.

To put our situation in context, the typical *youth* ministry professional often takes the opposite route, choosing from a wide array of undergraduate and graduate programs to train for the profession of youth ministry. Even those who do not get a formal education spend countless hours at high-energy continuing-education events or conferences, learning from experienced professionals in their field. When it comes to youth ministry, the temptation for churches is to look for the "superstar," someone with a sparkling personality who can easily draw young people into a youth group, attend endless sports events, and disciple multitudes of teenagers. But those who step into professional children's ministry (and the churches they serve) face an entirely different temptation all together.

The Parable of the Workhorse

Once upon a time, there was a farmer who had a small, well-kept farm. And on that farm he had some chickens. They were strong, healthy chickens and laid their eggs right on time, every time. He also had some goats who kept the grass well manicured, and some crops, a few rows of this and a few rows of that.

What the farmer and his family earned from selling the crops, eggs, and a little bit of goats' milk supported the family. The farmer began to look around at some of the other farms in the area. He saw that many of the farmers had at least one horse. He thought, *If we had a horse, we could expand our crops and make more money to support the family.* He scraped together his savings and went out to find a horse.

He found the perfect horse for the farm. She was a beauty; just watching her run in the pasture was enough to convince the farmer that she was the one. Her name was Sassie. She had previously been a show horse. She was a perfect equine overachiever.

The farmer only needed Sassie to pull the plow. Other than that, she would have plenty of room to run and enjoy the farm. He brought Sassie home, and showed her around the farm. She got connected to the plow, and started plowing.

Knowing that Sassie loved to run free in the pasture, the farmer often let her run free, which she loved. And she was so beautiful when she ran.

One thing led to another, and not only was Sassie pulling the plow but she had increased the size of the plot for crops. She made herself useful by pulling the family to town in a wagon, rounding up cattle, and helping to deliver the harvested crops to the market.

Everyone agreed. Bringing Sassie to the farm was the best decision they could have possibly made.

After many days of harvesting and carrying goods to the market, the farmer remembered how much Sassie loved to run. He led her to her favorite pasture. But Sassie felt tired. All she could think about was all the work she had left to do. *This is no time to run,* she thought.

The farmer saw a very different horse in the field. Her once beautiful gait was a labored walk. In the field, Sassie felt restless without a job to do. So she lay down to take a nap. As she dropped off to sleep, she began to feel sorry for herself, with just a hint of resentment, wishing so many people didn't expect so much from her so often.

The Problem with "I Can Do That"

Many of the children's ministry tasks are little ones, for which we naturally say, "I'll just take care of that." Need the bulletin board updated? I can do that. Need to post those pictures on Facebook? I can do that. Need to reserve the van for the fifth- and sixth-grade retreat? I can do that.

At first, we *can* do just about everything ourselves. We can prepare crafts and lessons each week. We can recruit a few volunteers when some drop out. We can create a training program when volunteers don't live up to our expectations.

Then, the fall festival sneaks up on us. The church is expecting something as exciting as last year's festival. So we make a list and start managing all the details. No need to put this burden on someone else. Maybe next year we can start earlier.

Then one fine fall day, as we are disinfecting toys in the nursery, the choir director comes in and asks what our plans are for the Christmas musical. We take it in stride, but it's late November. We've got no expertise in music, but hey, we like Christmas. We find a few cute songs, gets some motions off of YouTube, and get a few rehearsals on the calendar.

In the meantime, that wonderful couple who was teaching the first- through third-grade Sunday school class calls to say they are moving. We begin to feel like we're merely reacting, just trying to keep up with the treadmill on high speed. The idea of asking for help is oceans away. There is no time to explain what needs to be done.

And if we are not careful, we are in danger of being nibbled to death by a million tiny tasks. Because the tasks are so small, it feels silly to ask for help. And so we don't. We don't, that is, until we are so overwhelmed that we find ourselves saying no to things we ought to be saying yes to.

I've seen some of the most gifted children's ministers I know become so reactive that it would be comical if it weren't so sad. I was in a volunteer leaders' meeting with one of them not long ago. He was asked, "Could you call these three potential volunteers to see if they could help next year?" What could have been a collaboration-building "Sure, I'll reach out to them this week and get back to you next week," he said, "I *cannot* make one more phone call! People don't call me back. Someone else is going to have to make those calls!"

Um. Maybe not the best way to build the confidence of a volunteer team! The Workhorse Syndrome happens to children's ministers when they least expect it. While we are doing the work of the ministry, tending to the urgent and important, it becomes increasingly difficult to focus on building the systems that make delegating tasks successful. Planning ahead and building processes in which delegation actually works doesn't happen by accident. If we do not intentionally choose to build them, we have chosen not to build them.

When the point leader for children's ministry shoulders all of the work with very little help from a team, that leader has fallen victim to the Workhorse Syndrome. So, how do you know if you have fallen into the workhorse trap? Chances are, you already know, but just in case, the following are a few questions to help you know whether you (or someone you know) has become a workhorse.

The Workhorse in the Mirror

Over the years, working with lots of children's ministry professionals, I have observed a definite type. Though not everyone fits the mold, there's enough of a pattern that I think I can, with relative confidence, paint a picture of the typical children's pastor.

Commitment to get stuff done. When I began in children's ministry, I was amazed at what we could get accomplished, especially when we were under the gun with a surprise assignment.

Every now and then my boss could bring a last-minute directive about new way to operate the check-in process, or a special event that needed to be pulled together, or a last-minute change to the programming for the upcoming weekend. It can be difficult for me to change course once I'm moving forward on something. I may have forgotten to wear my joyful-spirit face when I was working on these last-minute expectations.

Almost every time, though, the thing I thought would have been impossible was up and ready by the time Sunday morning rolled around. I was amazed at what I could accomplish (even with an embarrassingly crummy attitude) when I finally decided to get onboard with each new idea.

If I knew that something would be good for the kids or would allow me to keep my job, there wasn't much I wouldn't do. I would stay up late, give up time with my husband, and forgo taking care of myself physically.

After working with children's ministers around the country, this type of get-it-done-no-matter-the-cost attitude is shared by the vast majority of us. And while a can-do attitude is exactly what we need to bring to our churches, we sometimes imagine that our only option is working in ways that sacrifice our families, our sanity, and ultimately our longevity in ministry.

Willing to burn the midnight oil. Sometimes part of "making it happen" means giving up some sleep. My most creative ideas often don't come three months in advance. Sometimes they come with less than twenty-four hours' notice! (Thank goodness that Walmart is always open!)

We do what has to be done to get those VBS decorations ready, get the Advent Fair crafts prepared, or the game props ready for Sunday morning. Sure, it would be nice to have some help, but we also know it would be rude to ask for help on such short notice.

So we get the job done, even if we have to do most of it ourselves. Of course, senior pastors love never having to worry about the children's ministry, knowing that every detail *will* be taken care of, even if it is just in the nick of time!

Hyper-responsibility. People who take responsibility for things *they* are not necessarily responsible for are hyper-responsible. Though they get a lot of work done, this pattern takes its toll on both the person taking too much responsibility and the one who is actually responsible.

Hyper-responsible children's ministers have trouble letting their volunteers *own* parts of the ministry. Too many children's ministry veterans feel like *they* have to purchase every goldfish, cut out every little lamb, and disinfect every infant toy. We know in our heads that our nursery volunteers could easily stay an extra five minutes to wipe down toys or throw them in the dishwasher, but we feel compelled to do it ourselves.

Do the math with me. It takes a volunteer team less than five minutes to get a room cleaned and set. It can take us as much as forty-five minutes every week to reset all the rooms. (Over the course of a year, that is the equivalent of almost three full workdays.) It's in the avalanche of simple tasks that we are most often tempted toward a hyper-responsibility. Because it is always easier (on the front end) to "just to do it ourselves," we wind up robbing the ministry of our time and energy that might be put to much more strategic use.

Before long, these three traits conspire to create the Workhorse Syndrome. The symptoms come on slowly, often so slowly they are hard to recognize. But one day the veteran children's worker looks in the mirror and sees

1. a loss of joy in ministry

2. lack of personal interests outside of church

3. no significant relationships outside of church or ministry

4. short-fuse frustration

5. exhaustion ("really, really, really tired")

6. feelings of isolation

7. a victim mentality ("There's really nothing I can do about . . .")

When the systems and organizational structures that allow the workload to be shared among a team are missing, the conditions are right for the building of a workhorse leader.

The workhorse syndrome affects high-capacity leaders who feel that every detail rests on their shoulders alone. Returning to what has worked so well in the past, they become hyper-responsible micromanagers who can't seem to let go of the anchor weighing them down. Eventually, they complain of being overworked, lonely, and burned out. Fortunately, this destination is completely avoidable.

What Only I Can Do

Without a sustainable systems in place and absolute clarity about what we will take personal responsibility for, we are destined to get loaded down with tasks that could be easily shared with our team. What if we changed our mantra from "I can do that" to "I'll do what only I can do"?

What are the things that "only I can do"? Here's a starting list:

1. Only I can tend to my joy in Christ.

2. Only I can lead my team.

3. Only I can align my team around a common direction.

4. Only I can take responsibility for building a great team.

5. Only I can create and protect the joyful culture of our children's ministry.

6. Only I can manage what I do with my time.

7. Only I can tend to my own emotional health, to the health of my marriage, and to my relationship with my own kids.

Sadly, too many children's ministry professionals neglect what only we can do in order to be excellent at the ministry minutiae someone else could handle. Our perfectionism about secondary things becomes a heavy burden.

Becoming a sustainable leader (and not just a workhorse) begins when we make the decision to be a different kind of leader. It begins with a decision to spend time on the parts of ministry only we can take care of. It begins with making a priority of gaining enough altitude to actually lead our ministries rather than be led by them. I know this may sound like it's beyond your reach, but the next few chapters will give you some practical steps that will help bring this dream closer to your reality.

Beyond Goldfish and Bubble Machines

A Different Way of Doing Children's Ministry

> *Put first things first and second things*
> *are thrown in. Put second things first and*
> *you lose both first and second things.*
>
> C. S. LEWIS, "GOD IN THE DOCK"

> *The words easy and adventure*
> *seldom travel together.*
>
> JON ACUFF, *DO OVER*

I can get downright giddy over the fun things we get to do in children's ministry. I can still remember the feeling I had when I got to purchase my first bubble machine for our preschool classrooms. I knew how excited our kids would be to walk into their class and into a cloud of bubbles.

In children's ministry there is no end to the games, crafts, and decorations. On Easter Sunday one year, we had life-size bunnies and duckies in costume. What's not to love about a job with life-size bunnies and duckies? It's just one of the perks of being in a ministry that uses every avenue imaginable to connect with kids in order to create the opportunity to introduce them to Jesus.

Often though, these creative ideas become *the* thing that parents and children remember about our ministry. And it is easy for these *wow* moments to be seen as the measuring stick for evaluating the success of our children's ministries. Everybody loves a little excitement and splash. But after a few laps around the children's ministry block, it doesn't take long to realize that many of these unforgettable moments are only the icing on a very complex cake.

Maybe you're like me—born with a sweet tooth. Maybe you've been known to eat dessert first every now and then. When I see a cake without icing, honestly, I feel a little sad deep down inside. You might have guessed it: yes, my favorite part of any cake is the icing.

So in honor of my sweet-toothed comrades, I give you a few fun facts about icing:

1. Icing can be used to make a cake beautiful.

2. Icing can be used to enhance a cake's sweetness.

3. Icing by itself, though, is just a shapeless blob of sugar; it's made to go *with* something else.

Sure, every now and then, I might want a single bite of leftover icing from the frosting bowl. But even I don't want more than a bite without something to go with it.

During my first go-round on a children's ministry staff, I'm embarrassed to admit that I spent the vast majority of my time on the icing parts of ministry. We had centerpieces on every table at every event, balloon arches, life-sized cutouts, and more themed T-shirts than I care to count!

But behind the scenes, I was constantly battling a whirlwind of chaos. Like trying to form a cake out of nothing but frosting, I found myself left with nothing but a sweet, sticky blob where I wanted a solid, sustainable ministry. I longed to build a grounded, healthy ministry, one that would stand the test of time without wearing out staff, volunteers, and parents. Without knowing what it was, I felt a hollowness about what we were doing. And I was exhausted and unsatisfied.

The Dance Floor

I knew I needed something more foundational to anchor my work. I was tired of my ministry being ruled more by the whirlwind of activities than by any clear direction. Something clicked for me when I read this parable of the dance floor from Mark DeVries.

Years of preparation had made her movements effortless, her turns seamless, her leaps weightless. A dancer of unparalleled talent, she mesmerized the crowd with her skill, but even more with her passion. Her countenance proclaimed in no uncertain terms that she was made for this moment.

But she would finish much sooner than anyone expected. Coming down from an arching leap, she landed with a jolting crack, her foot driving its way through the rotting wood of the floor, her body twisted in pain, her leg bent in places it was not made to bend. She was pulled from the stage, wondering if she would ever dance again.

The master of ceremonies dismissively apologized, "Inexperience does this to a dancer."

But no one repaired the floor. And then, as if nothing had happened, the next performer was introduced. The crowd responded with a smattering of applause but with no one attending to the dance floor, the audience knew that the new dancer would also find her performance ending prematurely with a disappointing, perhaps tragic, conclusion.

When I first read this parable, I found myself in tears. These were not the little misty-eyed, lump-in-the-throat tears, but big, boo-hooing, salty, sobbing, running-down-my-face kind of tears. I can be a little dramatic, I know.

But something about that story resonated deeply with me. I could hear the bone crack when the dancer fell. I could feel the break in her leg, because I too have been broken in ministry more than once.

I had dreamed of becoming a children's ministry "dancer" since I was a little girl. I wanted kids to know Jesus in the ways I had come to know him as a child. It seemed, though, that each time I began this ministry dance, I'd find myself on a cracked, broken, or rotting floor. I longed to do this work so badly, so, even knowing the risk, I'd keep going out on the dance floor again and again.

I would dance, full-out, until suddenly, as if out of nowhere, "Crack!" The floor would give way and something deep in my soul would break. I would hear the voices of judgment (including my own): "She must not have cared enough." "She just didn't have the right experience." "If she had really done her homework . . ."

How many times I considered myself unfit for the dance, thinking that the secret was to spend more time sharpening my own dancing skills and collecting a few more creative ideas. But my skills, admittedly incomplete, were not the problem. The problem was a rotting dance floor, which I totally ignored. Spending more time practicing my dancing skills could never solve the problem.

A Tale of Two Children's Pastors

Meet Amy. She loves Jesus, and she loves kids. She has been leading a children's ministry at her own church for over seven years, running at full speed ever since she can remember.

Her motto is, "If you want something done right, you have to do it yourself." Often referred to as the Energizer Bunny, Amy does whatever is required to get the job done. She remembers each volunteer's name and the names of their children after just one meeting. The church marvels at how much she has stored away in that ultraquick, filled-to-the-gills brain of hers.

Today, Amy is putting out the latest children's ministry fire. This week, she is dealing with volunteer and equipment issues. Volunteers are consistently inconsistent. For the last three weeks, one of the third grade Sunday school teachers has been MIA, without having given any notice. Amy spends most of her time dealing (quite efficiently) with some level of crisis.

While Amy hopes that the teacher is all right, her real concern is how she is going to replace this teacher for Sunday. At the same time, rumor has it that the kindergarten teachers have gone off the curriculum rails and are teaching whatever comes to mind. In the preschool class the video projector hasn't been working for a couple of weeks. Amy just found out about the projector this morning when a curt text arrived from a frustrated volunteer asking why the children's ministry can't get their act together with one simple projector.

Amy is thinking to herself, *How in the world can I fix a problem if I don't even know about it?* Amy rarely slows down long enough to take care of herself ("Who's got time?" she argues) or to tend to the multiple piles of paper on her desk. Her dream is that one day programs will run smoothly, volunteers will be responsible, she will get to enjoy a quiet Saturday night with her family, and get to bed before midnight.

Now, I want you to meet Catie. For the past five and a half years Catie has led a children's ministry across town from Amy. She has been hoping to meet Amy for lunch, but every time they had something on the calendar, Amy cancelled at the last minute with a frantic apology and a promise to make it up to Catie.

This week, Catie is planning the details for her volunteer training event for the next quarter. Specifically, she is working on creative ways of honoring her preschool volunteer coordinator as the Volunteer of the Year.

Her ministry isn't without its challenges, of course. Every Sunday, a regular volunteer gets sick or calls in with an unforeseen emergency. When it happens, Catie smiles and says, "Honey, that's what substitutes are for!" Catie's husband marvels at how consistently she is able to do her job with so many curve balls thrown at her and still come home with a smile on her face.

Every Tuesday, Catie does a walk through of each of her Sunday school classrooms, gathering individual incident report forms, classroom needs forms, and lesson feedback reports. She then heads to the kitchen, pours a cup of coffee, and settles into her office, enjoying her coffee as she reads through Sunday's paperwork and crafts her to-do list for the rest of the week.

In addition to planning her volunteer event, today Catie will make some recruiting calls, parent calls, and ask her supply coordinator to order craft supplies for the next quarter. Before Catie leaves for the day, she will complete a maintenance request to check the projector lightbulbs in the preschool rooms. At 4:45, Catie will head out to the door to watch her son play baseball.

While Amy and Catie are fictional characters, I'll bet you may have met at least one of them. Their stories reveal the difference between the all-too-common, do-it-yourself children's director managing all the details of ministry *herself* and the rare children's minister who builds and utilizes solid systems to manage her ministry.

I know what you're thinking. When you're dealing with an endless parade of immediate and urgent concerns, it's all you can do to react appropriately to those isolated incidents. It just feels more direct to do it yourself, right?

If you're like me, I'll bet you've heard these words come out of your mouth: "I would *love* to have time to work on bigger issues, but there are too many urgent demands screaming for my attention *right now!*"

I spent many years playing the role of Amy. In my Amy days, I would look at my different lesson plans for Sunday on Friday morning and make my shopping list for that afternoon.

On more weeks than I care to remember, I would find myself wandering around Target looking for something that couldn't be easily found in a regular big box store. Panic would set in.

Of course, these were the days before smartphones. You couldn't google anything. Siri wasn't around to answer my pressing question: *Where am I going to get flash paper at the last minute?*

I would get out the old yellow phone book, call around, and drive around until I found the magic store, which, of course, was closed on Friday night. I would drag myself into a house full of hungry people wondering what was taking dinner so long.

Eventually, I started making baby steps. Tired of the last-minute weekend scramble, I developed a plan for gathering all the fun supplies that did *not* involve a Friday night road trip to the magic store! Eventually, God blessed me with a volunteer who loved managing the supply piece (as long as I would promise never to ask her to teach).

More and more, I tried to live by the philosophy "Only do what only I can do." I found a friend gifted at editing curriculum, and she would look at each lesson and decide which of the suggested activities would best fit our church, facilities, budget, and kids. She would make a list of needed supplies. She would give me a month's worth of supply needs at a time, a month in advance, giving us at least four weeks to purchase, borrow, or find what we needed for any given Sunday.

Sure, there was a down side. This plan required more work on the front end. Switching gears from reacting to today's demands to thinking and planning more long term was hard. Living in a state of perpetual urgency was liberating at one level. I seldom had to think. By nature, I like to solve problems quickly and move on. That means I like to solve problems *myself*!

While it may have been easier in the short term just to deal with the immediate crises and get them off of my plate, in the long run, those same issues kept coming back and hijacking my schedule. I was living in the land I call "Short-term easy. Long-term hard."

As I have given myself the luxury of building systems, so many of the chronic, recurring urgencies have faded into the background. Let's call that "Short-term hard. Long-term easy." It's not rocket science, but it *is* hard work!

Both Amy and Catie had issues with video projectors. Amy was completely unaware for weeks that this was a problem. If part of the lesson she provided to volunteers included a video segment, there is no telling how long those volunteers may have been supplementing the lesson on the fly (and how quickly their frustration was growing, along with their mistrust of Amy's leadership).

Catie built a system that allowed volunteers to report when something was broken and implemented a preventative maintenance plan as well. A feedback form for classroom needs, along with properly trained volunteers, resulted in simple problems being solved before frustration had a chance to fester.

You'll remember that Catie also had a substitution system in place. She recognized the nature of family chaos and understood that life can dish out plenty of surprises to volunteers on a Sunday morning.

Why Systems Matter

Jesus said that his desire was that our "fruit . . . will last" (John 15:16). It wouldn't be a stretch to translate those words, "that our fruit should be sustainable." The right systems, like a good fence in a garden, can offer the kind of protection any ministry will need to thrive.

Up to this point, you've heard me use the word *systems* often. I've talked about the foundation of a ministry and some of the key processes. In the next chapters, we'll define what we mean when we talk about taking a systems approach to children's ministry.

Measuring Up

Knowing What It Takes

> *What we attend to flourishes.*
> *What we ignore withers.*
>
> ANONYMOUS

> *Perhaps the single most transformative moment*
> *of all is when a leader says, "I don't know what to do,"*
> *and then goes about the hard work of leading the*
> *learning that will result in a new faithful action.*
>
> TODD BOLSINGER, *CANOEING THE MOUNTAINS*

I love going to children's ministry conferences. I love meeting people as passionate about this work as I am.

True confession: For years, I went to children's ministry conventions with the secret hope that I would find *the* next great ministry idea. I jumped from balloon animals to bubble machines, from rotation models to puppet shows, from the hottest new speaker to the you've-never-seen-anything-like-*this*-before curriculum.

But a great conference can feel a little bit overwhelming—so much information, so many ideas, so many possible directions to pursue. So I've made it a habit, at the end of every conference, to identify my top two ideas—only two—to focus on when I get home.

If you've never tried to take three or four days of awesome material and narrow it down to just two big takeaways, you might be surprised how tough it is—especially for people who love new ideas! But without this kind of focus, I'm pretty sure I would attend conference after conference, spend lots of money, and wind up with nothing to show for it but a collection of notes I'd never look at again!

Of all the great ideas I have gathered, one of the greatest is this: *There is no singular good idea that will transform a struggling children's ministry into a sustainable, effective one.* In other words, the next great idea will be absolutely useless without the kind of systems required for building a faithful, thriving, manageable children's ministry.

Frequently changing direction based on the latest hot idea can be detrimental to our ministries. Every new direction requires time to work out the kinks. And bouncing from one great idea to another can prevent a ministry from getting traction. Churches that look for a quick fix to their children's ministry woes will soon find themselves exhausted and eventually stuck.

Balloon animals (and the million other "cutting-edge" ideas out there) will never be enough to transform our ministries. Solid children's ministries are based on something else altogether. So if we don't focus on ideas, what *do* we focus on? To borrow from the *Sound of Music*, "Let's start at the very beginning."

A Place to Start

Jesus told his disciples a story about an ambitious builder who wanted to erect a tower. He started building, never taking the time to determine what it would cost to complete the job (Luke 14:28-30). It didn't turn out well for him.

Building a thriving children's ministry begins at the place most churches avoid altogether: being crystal clear about what we want. Though it sounds simple, it may be the most challenging part of the process.

Here's the pattern we've seen. We ask the leaders of a particular church what they'd like to see in their children's ministry; more often than not, they say "more kids!" Okay, most don't *start* by saying more kids. They start—rightly so—with the desire to see children experience for themselves the love of Christ. But when we point out that this is very likely already happening, at least with a few kids, they eventually get to "more kids."

To these churches, more kids means reaching more people with Jesus' love, not just about having more kids than the church down the street. But when we ask, "How many more kids?" we see in the leaders' countenance, *That's got to be the dumbest question in the world!*

We push for an answer and hear, "Well, as many as we can get, of course!" Um, I'm going to have to say that's not an answer.

What if a school district tried to build a school building for as many kids as they can get? What if a professional football coach made a primary goal of getting as many players as possible on the team? What if a builder started with no other plan than to build it as big as possible?

But most children's ministries make that very mistake. They start building before deciding what size they want to be.

So let's start here. Do not pass go until you've decided the capacity you'd like to have for your ministry.

The decision-making process starts with collecting information.

* How many children and children's families are in your database?

* How many children are participating in some way in the life of the church in an average week?

* What are we currently spending on our children's ministry?

* How does that investment break down in terms of cost per child per week?

* Do we have any more staffing hours, volunteer hours, or finances to invest?

Once you've gathered that information, you can compare it to some national norms. Fortunately, Ministry Architects has discovered a few patterns that can provide a baseline that you can benchmark your own children's ministry against.

Though these ratios are not statistically precise (these numbers do not come from academically refereed studies), we have good reason to believe that they can provide an accurate and faithful baseline for your church to consider its investment. Please remember that these numbers don't guarantee health in a ministry. These are merely norms, meaning that many ministries see success with different levels of investment; however, the norms serve as a good way to see where your church falls in comparison with churches around the country. In working with churches of all different sizes, denominations, and complexities of programming, we've discovered these four patterns:

$1,000 per child. A good rule of thumb is that for every $1,000 a church invests annually in children's ministry, it can expect to see one child participating on an average week. (There are a number of variables that can affect this ratio—geography, cost of living, size of the church, and so forth.) At first, this sounds like a pretty high number, but when you take a closer look at every dollar spent on the children in your church, you will see that the numbers add up quicker than you might imagine. Your actual line-item budget might not reflect this number, but the church may be spending more money on its children than what is stated in the children's ministry budget. For example, if the choir director spends eight hours a week on children's choir, you would add 20 percent of the choir director's salary

and benefits into money spent on children in your church. Add to that the cost of goldfish, diaper wipes, curriculum, photocopies, nursery equipment, and background checks, and the dollar signs begin to accumulate.

For example, with an annual budget of $25,000, a church can expect to have an average weekly participation of around twenty-five children each week. The financial investment includes the children's ministry's program budget as well as staff salaries and benefits. Program budget includes everything from spare diapers to VBS decorations.

One wild card for many churches is paid nursery workers. Because there is extraordinary variety in what churches pay nursery workers, this number may have an impact on the $1,000 per child ratio.

Why does all this detail about money and ratios even matter? Churches that underfund their children's ministries are often surprised to find volunteers, parents, and staff who feel discouraged, undervalued, and disgruntled. Churches trying to save a few dollars on their children's ministry often shoot themselves in the foot, creating a kind of negative climate around the children's ministry that repels new people and frustrates even the most faithful parents.

Does this mean that less affluent churches cannot have a sustainable children's ministry? Not at all. Those churches simply need to match their investment to their expectations. If they have funding for five kids, they can create a marvelous ministry for those five!

One full-time staff person for every seventy-five children. The way a church staffs its children's ministry can be a great indicator of the value the church places on this ministry. A typical church will have the equivalent of one full-time staff member for every seventy-five kids who participate in some aspect of the ministry each week.

For example, a church that hopes to have thirty-five children active on an average week can probably get by with a half-time children's director. A church that hopes to have 225 children on an average week will need three full-time children's staff people.

In calculating this number, you'll want to include the total number of staff hours allotted to the children's ministry. So if the music minister dedicates five hours a week to children's choir, those hours are included in the total number of children's ministry staff hours the church is providing. Here's another way to think of it: for every seventy-five kids participating on an average week, the church needs to dedicate forty staff hours to keeping the children's ministry running at a healthy pace.

At this point, we often hear this objection: "But what if we have more volunteers?" Apart from someone to coordinate the work of the volunteers, those volunteers will simply not stick around. They will be frustrated by the lack of support, by conflicting visions with other volunteers, and by the sense that serving in the children's ministry can feel like a "life sentence." For a group larger than a handful of kids, someone needs to be the point person, responsible for being the hub of the ministry and keeping all its components in good working order.

One adult volunteer for every five children. Another rule of thumb is to have one adult volunteer for every five children. Accordingly, you'll want to take the total number of children participating on an average week and divide it by the number of volunteers serving weekly in your ministry. For example, if you've got thirty-five children and five volunteers on an average week, you have a ratio of one adult to every seven children.

Because one adult can successfully pay attention to about five children, we have observed that healthy children's ministries have a ratio of one adult to about five children. If you've got rotating volunteers (not a best practice), you would use the number of volunteers serving on an average week. For example, if you have teaching teams of four people who each serve once a month, you would count that team as one weekly volunteer, not four. We might even consider four volunteers rotating in and out every week to be less than one person since they have much less opportunity to actually *know* the children and their families. (If you're already struggling to hang on to the adults you've got, feel free to jump to chapter seven on recruiting volunteers.)

If you have questions about how many adults are *required* to care for babies, toddlers, and older kids, you can check your state's guidelines for daycare. Sure, the children's ministry is *not* daycare, but those standards can be a helpful for ensuring the safety of your children.

Fifteen percent of the worshiping congregation. In a typical church, the number of children who participate weekly in some type of program at the church tends to settle around 15 percent of the total number of people who worship on an average week.

So, if fifty people participate in worship on an average weekend, you can expect seven or eight children to participate in the life of the church. If one thousand people worship at your church on the weekend, you can expect somewhere in the neighborhood of 150 children to participate in your ministry on an average week. We know that churches can vary widely in their demographics. However, we have seen churches with significantly older congregations, who desire to minister to kids and who choose to make the appropriate investment in the systems and processes of sustainable children's ministry, successfully incorporate more children into their ministry.

Of course, this number can vary widely, and all four of these norms work collectively. For example, a church of three thousand in worship may have just two hundred children involved on an average week, but they are also not investing in staff and volunteers at a rate that would be required for a healthy ministry to 450 (15 percent). Or a church of 150 in worship may find themselves with over forty children involved weekly because of a long-term full-time staff person with great volunteers.

What's Your Capacity?

I'm not saying you should spend more money on your children's ministry. I'm saying you should match your expectations to your investment. If you've only got the funds to faithfully engage ten children, then your church's leadership needs to be crystal clear that they have decided to have ten children involved (and be happy about it). One surefire way to suck the energy out of a children's ministry is to invest at one level and expect results that are twice (or ten times) as much as the investment would merit.

When George began as the Christian education director at his church, he was energetic and passionate. People were amazed at his energy. Now, after just two years in his position, he seems on edge more often than not. What started as a joy has begun to feel more like a prison he endures "for the sake of the children." He was stopped short recently when his youngest daughter asked, "Daddy, when did you grow those angry eyes?"

It's easy to blame pastors, parents, or congregants. But upon closer inspection, you'll likely find what we call a crisis of capacity. This sounds pretty nonthreatening, but don't be fooled. It is the cause of so much toxicity and dysfunction in so many churches.

Here's a way to think about it. Imagine I'm planning a trip from sunny Texas to New York City for Thanksgiving. I have a brand new suitcase, and I'm excited to take it on its first trip.

I have packed enough to keep me well-dressed for my four-day trip. Everything is humming along smoothly until I get to step five, "Closing the Suitcase." It just won't zip. I try sitting on it. It doesn't work.

I bring in my husband to sit on it. It still won't zip. My blood pressure is going up. As I am stomping around the house, my husband points out that this particular suitcase has an extra zipper that can expand its capacity 4 to 6 inches. (I hate it when he's right, even in imaginary stories.) It works! I unzip that handy little zipper, and suddenly my shower gel and running shoes have room to breathe. What a relief!

I can relax. I'm excited about the trip again. But then it hits me. I forgot a coat! No one goes to New York for Thanksgiving without a coat! But there's absolutely no room left in my suitcase. Panic sets in again.

What's my problem? I have a crisis of capacity. I have a choice to make: spend Thanksgiving in New York without a coat, or get a larger suitcase. This suitcase simply does not have the capacity to get the job done.

Here's another way to think about it. If you are a children's ministry staff person, you are hired for a finite number of hours a week. In addition to those hours, you do an impressive job juggling things like housekeeping, bill paying, eating, sleeping, caring for your family, maintaining friendships, and keeping your body and soul healthy.

All the while, it is easy for church members, parents, boards, and committees to assume that you should be able to accomplish everything the church needs in the allotted time. The problem is that programs, responsibilities, and relationships are being added to your ministry suitcase. It just won't fit.

Every now and then a church calls our Ministry Architects team to help with a general sense of disorganization or lack of direction in their children's ministry. One of our discoveries over the years is that in many instances simply replacing the "disorganized" staff person with someone "more organized" doesn't really solve the problem.

The problem may not be with organization at all but with a crisis of capacity. When a church expects more results than their investment can produce, that church will see a contagion of blaming, advice giving, and discouragement, none of which really moves the needle.

It's when a children's ministry balances its resources and its expectations that we have a solid starting point for building a thriving ministry. When these are in balance, anxiety dissipates, creativity blossoms, and everyone begins to relax and get to work.

It can be hard to talk about money for children's ministry. In most churches, there is little sense of urgency about children's ministry. A leaky roof in a church creates a sense of urgency. A broken air conditioner in a Texas summer creates an immediate action. But underinvestment in children's ministry is accepted in many churches as something we'll just have to live with. However, the high cost of the discomfort of living without air conditioning doesn't hold a candle to the cost of burnout, frustration, and loss of members created by chronic underinvestment in children's ministry.

The Job You Didn't Know You Had

If you are tempted to put this book down right now and run to your finance committee to prove that your ministry is underfunded and understaffed, you might want to first think a little more deeply.

Before you launch a campaign to go after your church's finance committee, remember that every church has to make choices. After all, there are only so many resources to go around. There is a good chance that those making the financial decisions in the church value children and know that having a thriving children's ministry is essential to the church's long-term health.

Why, then, are most children's ministries underfunded? Sometimes it looks like this. A mom (let's call her Stacy) is one of those "rock star" volunteers who was asked a year or two ago to coordinate the children's ministry because "there is no one else to do it." With a passion for kids, a love for Jesus, and a large carton of Goldfish crackers, Stacy enters the world of ministry.

Juggling supply lists, volunteer emails, curriculum decisions, and *lots* of meetings, she is determined to make children's ministry experience a great one for the kids in her church. As a high-capacity mom, she is used to shouldering a heavy load of unrelated responsibilities for her family, and she does the same thing in her volunteer roles. She is so careful about money that she is admired for her frugality.

Naturally, in her ministry work, she rarely asks for help, especially when it comes to money. What Stacy doesn't realize is that if she doesn't champion the children's ministry cause, it is unlikely that her ministry will obtain the kind of funding support it needs to thrive. Quietly and faithfully shouldering the load alone likely will not move the ministry forward.

In most congregations, children's ministry can be "out of sight, out of mind." It's not that people don't care. But unless someone is a parent or a children's ministry volunteer, there's a good chance they'll never set foot in a children's ministry classroom. Sure, they may see VBS decorations once a year or walk past a colorful bulletin board, but they will naturally assume that until they hear otherwise the children's ministry has everything it needs.

If Stacy stays quiet and waits for the church leadership to figure out what the children's ministry needs, she will likely be waiting for a long time. We've seen way too many exhausted children's directors grow resentful and complain about the church's lack of support. Little do they know how much power they really have.

Once Stacy recognizes that it is part of her job to speak up and advocate for the needs of the children's ministry, she can be as intentional about communicating those needs as she is about her VBS programming. With a spirit of humility and gratitude, she can share the stories of the life-changing work happening in the church's children and their families.

She can figure out how budgeting decisions get made (committees and staff people need to be consulted). And she can make the case for the church appropriately investing in its future through the children's ministry. Though it may not produce immediate fruit in the current budget cycle, it is very likely that after a few years of working her plan to advocate for the children's ministry, she will see significant results.

If you are the point leader for your church's children's ministry, it all starts with recognizing that you are responsible not just for the day-to-day programming of the ministry but also for insuring that the church's expectations match their investment.

No one else in the church thinks about its children's ministry and what it needs as much as you do. If you don't sing this song, no one else will. And you won't likely get the support you need to run a sustainable children's ministry.

You may start out as the sole champion for the children's ministry in your church, and you may wonder, *Why doesn't the pastor or the youth minister or the music director champion children's ministry?* I know I had those thoughts more than once. They have young kids. They know how much it matters to their family. Why was I the only one banging this drum?

I did not realize that it wasn't just because they have their own causes. It was primarily because I never asked! I could have said, "John, in staff meeting today, would you mind sharing a little about how our take-home devotions last month affected your family?" I could have had everyone on our staff write down the name of a child "on their hearts" so I could pray for them. After one month, I could give them back, let them write a prayer update, and then redistribute them so they could pray for each other's children.

The Cart and the Workhorse

At one level, it is easy to throw money at a problem, assuming that more cash will solve any difficulty. When a relationship is rocky, we might purchase a gift. When we feel guilty for the time we aren't spending with an estranged family member, we might send a little bit nicer Christmas present. It's simple.

So it's tempting to take the same approach in ministry. Churches who want to attract young families decide that to compete with big churches with big budgets they need to invest in the bells and whistles, rather than identifying investments that can make a ministry unique and inviting, both to church families and those in the community.

Let's say your church wants to boost Sunday school attendance. The bustling ministry across town has a sparkling indoor playground and coffee shop teeming with young families. But an upgrade in facilities alone will do very little to revive a struggling ministry. Believe me, we've seen plenty of lousy children's ministries in awesome facilities.

As one piece of the puzzle, your church will definitely need facilities for children that feel safe for parents and inviting for kids. But expensive facilities are not the right starting place. Allow me to play devil's advocate.

Let's say that your major facilities upgrade brings in dozens of new families to check out the church. Is your children's ministry ready? Are there processes in place to connect with those families and integrate them into the life of the church? Are there processes in place to communicate a compelling vision for your ministry?

An indoor playground won't recruit, train, and inspire the volunteers you don't yet have. Colorful murals won't support parents in the faith development of their children. Don't fall into the trap of trying to put up wallpaper before pouring a strong foundation.

I love developing engaging, creative, and well-designed children's spaces! But our ministry becomes a cheap, flimsy imitation when we focus our first energy and resources on "wallpaper," while ignore major cracks in the foundation.

Here in Texas, when the soil doesn't get the moisture it needs, the foundations of buildings begin to crack. And those cracks have a way of showing up in the rest of the house, which is unsightly.

I have seen massive cracks in walls, from floor to ceiling, some wide enough to fit your finger in. Doorframes are no longer level. Floor tiles crack. I'll never forget the night our family was awakened by a cracking tile. It is so loud we thought we had just heard a gunshot!

It doesn't take a construction expert to know what would happen if we used beautiful and expensive wallpaper to cover up the cracks. Here are a few ways we've seen churches invest in wallpaper before they attended to their foundation:

* repainting classrooms before they have recruited enough teachers

* adding bubble machines to their preschool classrooms before determining the core competencies for their ministry

* redesigning the website when they still don't know the names of the children they serve

* purchasing bounce houses before the volunteers are equipped and understand their job descriptions

* hiring an artist to paint murals in the hallway before the calendar is published for the year

In the short run, it's almost always more fun to hang wallpaper and buy cute furniture than to tend to the foundation. As we turn to the next chapter, I'll unpack for you exactly what I mean when I use words like *systems*, *structures*, and *foundations*, and how those terms can be translated into the first steps toward a thriving, long-term, sustainable children's ministry.

Building Your Ministry with Simple Machines

The Essential Systems for a Sustainable Children's Ministry

Clutter fosters mediocrity.

THOM RAINER AND ERIC GEIGER,
SIMPLE CHURCH

*Walk with me and work with me—watch how I
do it. Learn the unforced rhythms of grace.*

MATTHEW 11:29, *THE MESSAGE*

E very ministry goes through stuck seasons, seasons when we've
stopped moving forward, seasons when we feel like we might
be moving backward. If you've been in children's ministry for even
a little while, there's a good chance you've experienced more than
one of these:

* You've lost a few key volunteers, and every weekend is now an
epic struggle to have enough adults for all your classes.

* You've started combining classes more often than not. Some weeks it seems like the only way to spread out the limited number of volunteers you have.

* You're concerned about the long-term effect on kids continually lumped into wide age spans and taught by a different teacher each week.

* You're seeing a climate of negativity among your staff or volunteers, to such an extent that the ministry feels more like a chore than a joy.

* The visitors you do have seldom stick around.

* Even your regular families have stopped coming so regularly.

* You're finding it impossible to meet the expectations of growing your ministry with a shrinking budget.

* Your own enthusiasm for the children's ministry is waning as you overhear rumblings, "concerns" about the children's ministry.

I've been in every one of those spots. When we come to a stuck place, we've got a choice. We can react by trying harder to do what we've always done. We can get hyperfocused on treating the symptoms of the problem (like sending out a challenging email to our volunteers, reminding them how important *commitment* is). Or we can get below the immediate problem and tend to the systems (or lack of systems) that are creating the problems in the first place. Here's what I mean.

Simple Is the New Strong

Remember in grade school when you started learning about simple machines—levers, pulleys, wedges, and inclined planes? These devices might appear inconsequential, but according to *Dictionary.com* a *simple machine* has the power to change "the magnitude or direction of a force." In other words, with the right machine, you will put forth less effort and accomplish more.

Have you ever tried to pull a nail out of a board with your bare hands? It's almost impossible. Well, I know a little secret that will save your hands from such trauma. The backside of a hammer has two little wedges that will lift that nail out of the board lickety-split. Those little wedges are a perfect example of how a simple machine can multiply force.

In this chapter, I want to introduce you to a few "simple machines" for children's ministry, systems that have the power to transform the magnitude and direction of all your hard work. With the right ministry machines, you can multiply the time and energy you are now spending on building volunteers, visitor retention, and budgeting.

We'll start with the foundational machines that every children's ministry needs:

* database

* calendars

* volunteer recruiting and equipping plan

I'll bet you just got a sinking feeling in your stomach when you read this list, didn't you? I know what you're thinking: *I can barely keep my head above water now. How in the world am I going to find time to develop all these big plans?*

Don't worry. We are going to work through each of these simple machines one at a time. Here's what you'll discover: you are already spending time in many, if not all, of these areas. But there's a good chance that your efforts in most of these areas is not a part of a large system, not a part of a machine that integrates, simplifies, and expands your impact.

That is the result we want to work toward in this chapter. The reason so few children's ministry professionals build these systems is that there is almost never an urgent need to do so. But the lack of systems results in an explosion of dozens (sometimes hundreds) of urgent and immediate tasks that must be tended to *now!* These systems won't prevent all emergencies, but they will keep you from spending all your time reacting to the latest fire.

The Database Machine

An organization that hopes to grow and build momentum will need an accurate, updated list of everyone involved in the ministry and those potentially involved: children, parents, volunteers, visitors, staff, and outside resources. You might be thinking: *Hey, we've only got ten children in our group. I can keep that information in my head.*

Really? If you've got a group of less than ten children, you *might* be able to remember their names, their parents' names, their age and grade in school, their birthdays, their addresses, phone numbers, email addresses, and food allergies, but why try? Why not follow Einstein's advice and "never memorize something you can look up"?

When we ask the average children's ministry professional about the accuracy and usefulness of their databases, it usually doesn't take more than sixty seconds to hear all the excuses for why this list isn't in good shape. Until you've got your list of children, families, and volunteers just the way you like it, do not delegate this task to someone else.

This is so important that I'll say it again. Please, do not delegate this task to someone else. I can't tell you how many children's ministry directors are *waiting* for someone else to get their lists right.

This is one that you, as the point leader, must take responsibility for. Like squaring the corners on a building, if your database is shaky, you're whole ministry will be. Some things are better *not* left to software.

Great news! You don't have to wait. And you don't have to be a computer expert either. You can take care of this yourself (and usually in pretty short order).

Start by deciding on a format that works for you. Some people use a different 3 x 5 card for every child. Some use an Excel spreadsheet. Some use a legal pad. Some use database management software. Some type the information out in a Word document. The key is to get it into a format that is *accessible* for you. The point is having a place from which you can easily *pull* information when you need it.

Once you've got the whole list of children, make sure you include

* address

* phone number

* parents' names

* parents' email addresses

* birthday and year

* year of graduation from the children's ministry (easier to keep up with than their grade in school or class assignment, which will change each year)

* food allergies or other health notes

* member status (member family, regular visitor family, new visitor family)

* school

Once you've gathered basic information for every child, include the same kind of information on every volunteer or potential volunteer. If you're using an Excel spreadsheet, you can create a separate tab for volunteers. If you're using a Word document, you can create a separate page for volunteers. If you're using 3 x 5 cards, you could use different colors for children and volunteers. You get the idea.

Gathering all this information will take a little time, especially if the information in your church's database is unreliable. But it won't take nearly as much time as waiting around for someone else to get it done!

Keep at it. There are few things that will affect the long-term stability of your ministry more than knowing your flock in this very deliberate way. As you get better at this process, it will become much easier.

Don't get discouraged if your first system or two ends up not working the way you like. Consider those first few attempts beta tests in the process of finding what works for you. Learn a lesson from Apple—make next year's iPhone a little better than this year's.

Three other recommendations:

* We recommend that you do a full database update at the same time every year. (I like summertime for this.)

* Every year, once you have updated your database, work with the person managing the church's database to make sure all the updates you have made make it into the church's overall system. At this point, you will have the most up-to-date information on these families, and the families will (rightly) assume that if information has been given to one staff member, the information has been given to the church.

* With the information you've gathered, you will be able to pull all the specific directories, such as

  o all the 1–3 graders

  o all the parents

  o all the volunteers

As an example, you can find a sample database (see "Children's Ministry Printed Directory") in the online resources for this book (ivpress.com/sustainable-children-s-ministry).

The Calendar Machine

Your database serves as a tangible reminder that your ministry is first about *who*, not just *what* and *when*. Once you've got your database in place (or even while you're getting it fully updated), it's time to create your programming calendar for the coming year. This foundational practice is, sadly, one of the most commonly procrastinated tasks in children's ministry.

It's totally understandable. There are so many more urgent programming and pastoral needs than the strategic, forward-moving tasks; they feel so mundane and often get pushed to the back burner.

Before you recruit one volunteer, before you ask for one dollar for your ministry, and before you expect one child to show up for your program, you need to have some dates nailed down. We've made it a standard practice at Ministry Architects churches to have every children's ministry publish a twelve-month calendar. When parents have this information early in the school year (or even before), you have greatly increased the chances of having the participation you are looking for.

I am going to go so far as to say that there is no reason for not having a published twelve-month calendar other than a lack of discipline. In our experience it probably won't take more than a couple of hours to gather the information you need and complete the calendar. If you're still waiting for some information from schools or other staff people, go ahead and draft your calendar, noting the places where the dates are subject to change if new information necessitates it.

The return on that two-hour investment can be staggering. You will save yourself all the lag time that comes when you have to answer questions with "We'll have to table that decision until we have a date set." You will also infuse trust and confidence among your parents and your staff colleagues. Yes, there is a chance that some will be annoyed that you are working so far ahead, but most will be impressed!

A published twelve-month calendar is a huge gift to your families. Parents plan their lives around sports calendars, school calendars, job deadlines, career commitments, and community events. If you don't get your calendar into their hands, the best you can expect from families is their leftovers.

So, the next time you are tempted to complain that families are choosing sports or other events over church events, remember that schools and city leagues typically give families more to work with when they distribute their calendars well in advance of our last-minute bulletin announcements. What would happen if your families received their church calendars first? What do you have to lose?

Once your calendar is created, share it in draft form first with the church staff for their input. Once it has been cleared on the church calendar, make a plan to get it in the hands of parents and volunteers. (Your fall kick-off event is a great time for this, if not earlier.)

The Volunteer Machine

For many children's ministries, the number-one challenge is staffing all of our programs and events with the appropriate number and the right kind of volunteers. It is rare to go into a church to talk about children's ministry and *not* hear the director lament the lack of volunteers.

More often than not, the problem is that there is no plan. Begging your pastor to make a plea from the pulpit is not a plan. Putting an announcement in the bulletin is not a plan. Tackling unsuspecting parents in the hallway is not a plan.

What every healthy children's ministry must have is a step-by-step plan for recruiting volunteers. How are you asking? Who are you asking? And when are you asking?

Once you have a plan that is working effectively, then (and only then) should you try to enlist others to help you recruit. Most children's directors try to delegate responsibility for recruiting, and the results fall somewhere between disappointing and disastrous.

Especially as you are building the foundation of your ministry, *you should be the one to work the plan.* Dividing up the list of names among your committee will only multiply your frustration and reinforce the (mistaken) belief that recruiting volunteers is next to impossible.

I know what you're thinking: *But we've always asked our children's ministry committee to do the recruiting.* As one talk show host says, "How's that workin' for you?"

If you're using your volunteers to recruit others and you've got all the inspired, aligned, and effective volunteers you need, feel free to continue this process. Sing the doxology and keep doing what you're doing! But only one out of one hundred churches experiences this.

Too often we have seen recruiting delegated to a committee, which often leaves vacancies in the volunteer roster and insufficient time for the director to fill them. Recruiting can be intimidating, so volunteers (like most of us facing an unpleasant task) tend to procrastinate, resulting in the all-too-common narrative, "We just can't get enough volunteers."

In chapter eight, we will outline a recruiting plan that consistently works in those churches that work the plan. Of course, once you have your volunteers, they will need training, coaching, and support to grow into their roles. Our responsibility doesn't stop when we plug their name into a spreadsheet.

You're probably thinking, *I've already asked so much of them, I can't ask them to come to another meeting!* I know. You may think you are giving a gift by not asking them to come to another meeting. In fact, you are robbing them of the energizing support that comes with being a part of a team that shares the same vision, and you are multiplying the chances of frustration and volunteer burnout.

Think of it this way: when someone signs up to volunteer at a hospital, homeless shelter, or school, they always receive some sort of training. Why do churches get everyone signed up, send them a lesson plan, and turn them loose in a room full of kids? (And we wonder why they don't want to sign up next year!)

A volunteer should never be shocked by how difficult their role is going to be. In fact, they should be so well prepared that they will leave each week knowing that (1) they are making a huge difference in the lives of children and families and (2) the job was a lot easier than expected.

When we fail to train our volunteers, we send the message that the job they signed up for isn't really that important; it is so simple and clear that training would be a waste of time. A great training plan communicates that we believe our volunteers' jobs really matter. They are not "helping us" with *our* ministries. They are on the front lines, doing the work of ministry, cultivating a new generation of disciples of Jesus Christ.

Of course, beyond formal training meetings, you have the opportunity (and responsibility) to care for and nurture your volunteers. In a sustainable ministry, your volunteers are *your* first flock, and the volunteers have the children as their flock.

There are plenty of creative ways to provide training and support for your team without overwhelming them with meetings. So stop apologizing for recruiting and training.

When you work a plan to train, nurture, and equip your volunteers, don't be surprised to see your volunteers coming back to serve year after year, and describing their children's ministry work one of the most life-giving experiences of their lives.

These three systems—database machine, calendar machine, and volunteer machine—represent the systems you'll want to get in place as a starting point. In chapter six, I'll introduce you to the systems you'll want to get in place next. But like a good triage nurse, you know you can't take care of building all these systems at once. Start with the three in this chapter. The others will require these three as a foundation, so start here.

From Pearls to a Necklace

Putting the Pieces Together

> *Mystification is simple; clarity is the hardest thing of all.*
>
> JULIAN BARNES, *FLAUBERT'S PARROT*

> *The truth is, mediocrity is natural. You don't have to do anything to drift there. It just happens.*
>
> MICHAEL S. HYATT, *PLATFORM*

Though he's been a pastor for thirty years, my coauthor, Mark, says he wasn't really "the preaching kind." Once or twice a year he would be asked to bring the message to his church, but for the most part his Sunday mornings were occupied by assisting in worship and leading his church's youth ministry.

Mark's been known to tell a funny story or two in his sermons. And it's not unusual to hear a catch in his voice when he's talking about kids, which he seemed to find a way to do in almost every sermon.

One Sunday after worship, a wise elder in the church, a retired Navy admiral, waited until the rest of the congregation had the chance to greet Mark. And once the way was clear, he took Mark's hand, looked him in the eye and said, "You had some real pearls there, Marcus." As the admiral turned to walk away, he said, with a twinkle in his eye, "Yep, some real pearls. I'm still looking for the string, but you had some real pearls in there!"

We have yet to visit a children's ministry that doesn't have "some real pearls." Maybe there's the mural in the children's wing that all the kids came together to paint a few years back. Maybe it's that grandmother serving in the nursery, who has been at her post for long enough to hold the babies of the babies she helped raise. Maybe it's a wonderful volunteer who sends out a weekly newsletter to parents with take-home activities that families actually *use*.

Every children's ministry has some real pearls. But most are lacking the string that keeps every component of the ministry in working order. In chapter five, I introduced you to key systems *every* children's ministry must have working in proper order as a foundation. Now I want to introduce you to the remaining systems that healthy, thriving sustainable youth ministries tend to regularly.

The Communication Machine

If you have been in children's ministry for even a little while, by now you have discovered how hard it is to keep everyone—parents, volunteers, staff—up to date and informed. How many times have we heard, "I didn't know about . . ." referring to an event that had been in the bulletin, newsletter, and on the website for months? It's enough to make you want to pull your hair out in frustration and scream, "What else do they want me to do!?"

Here's the bad news: there is no machine that can ensure that everyone will always get, much less read, every message we send. Our pace of life means that we skim and skip the majority of what comes in our inbox or mailbox. It's just a matter of survival for busy families.

So we build our communication system around this reality: just because we've sent something or published something we can never assume that the message has been received. When it comes to communications, our job is to make the lives of parents and volunteers as easy as possible. Of course, this is no easy task.

Some parents want things in the mail. Others prefer texts. Others are email only. And for some, only a phone call will do.

Here's the great news: we've got a simple machine that will solve more than 90 percent of your communication challenges.

1. Get all the essential information posted online. Parents and volunteers need a single place to go to find answers to questions: When does Sunday school begin? Where is the nursery? When are we doing VBS next summer? Eventually, you can put all this information in print, but you'll want it (and your families will need it) on the website first.

Make sure the children's ministry section of your church's website has all this essential information:

* Starting times and locations of all weekly programs.

* Children's ministry events calendar for the next twelve months. *Don't assume that your church's twelve-page master calendar containing every church committee meeting and room reservation is going to help!* Parents need a one-page list of key dates with starting and ending times, not a dozen pages filled with information they're not looking for.

* Brief instructions for families visiting for the first time, with information about where to come and what to expect.

* Information about how to sign up a child for every major event in the coming year, ideally each with a link to a signup page.

* Expectations for parents
  * pickup and drop-off times
  * sign-in processes
  * how to volunteer
  * children and the Lord's Supper
* Brief descriptions of all children's ministry programs
  * Sunday school
  * young children in worship (e.g., Are children dismissed during worship? At what age do children stay for the whole service?)
  * each special event
  * children's music programs
* Information about any rites of passage that fall under the children's ministry, including milestones such as
  * confirmation
  * baptism
  * first Bible
* Information about your church's requirements for volunteers working with children, including expectations such as
  * successful completion of a background check
  * a two-adult rule
  * completion of training
* A number to call or an email address where questions can be sent.

Once you get this foundational content created the first time, you'll need to update it at least once a year. And you should update the information and photos on your website at least monthly. Embarrassingly, the average church website takes a one-and-done approach, as if their information never needs to be updated. When a family looks on your website and sees that it is announcing dates for last year's event, it's not going to inspire a lot of confidence.

The annual updates, of course, will take much less time than gathering all the information the first time! Having all your content in one place will make it much easier to get specific content into the hands of the people you're trying to communicate with.

2. If you want an answer, don't use a billboard or a bulletin. A staff person at a large church told with me how frustrated she was with her congregation: "I sent a message out to three thousand people and only two responded."

An important lesson about communication in your ministry is that if you want a response, if you need volunteers, if you want someone to attend an event, you've got to get more personal than a group email or bulletin announcement. Long gone are the days when we could get all the volunteers we need by passing around a notepad in a worship service. If you want fifty people to attend the church picnic, your best bet is to line up four people to call or email twenty-five people each and collect definite responses. I'm not talking about a group call from a machine or a group email or text. I'm talking about something like this:

Hi Janie,

We're having our all-family picnic in two weeks on July 17 on the church grounds. We would love for you and your family to be there!

Any chance we'll get to see you?

Blessings,
Annette

If your church is typical, it will sometimes take three to four tries before you get an answer. But in today's information-saturated world, this is the only way your communication efforts will influence people's participation. You make your information available through fliers and your website. You change behavior by making specific asks.

3. Be redundant again. Some experts say that, on average, a person needs to be exposed to the same message seven times before it begins to sink in. So share information about your ministry in as many formats as possible: email, website, Facebook, Twitter, snail mail, bulletin boards, text messages, newsletter and bulletin announcements, and sometimes announcements in worship.

4. Develop a plan. Once you've got your calendar clear, you'll want to develop a game plan for how you'd like to promote the handful of programs most important to your ministry. For example, for your annual Easter egg hunt or VBS you might want to find ways to reach out to your community through the newspaper or fliers in mailboxes. For weekly programming, you'll promote differently. And volunteers will need an entirely different rhythm of communication all together.

If this isn't your strong suit, feel free to reach out to us at Ministry Architects, and we can help you put a plan together in pretty short order. We've included a sample communication plan in appendix A to help you get started.

Tracking the Who: Your Attendance Tracking Machine

If we're not careful, our ministries can revolve around *what* rather than *who*, the children and families that our ministries actually exist for. We've got programs to run, fliers to create, meetings to attend—all part of *what*. Keeping up with *who* can take some initiative, especially if you don't have a system in place for attendance tracking. It all starts with the question, Who *belongs* to us?

Once you've got your database machine humming, you'll be able to pull a directory of children and families who are "yours." Your directory is ordinarily made up of your active members and visitors. (We define an active member, for directory purposes, as someone whose family is a member of the church and who has participated at least once in the previous year.)

We recommend that you start with a printed directory in August of every year, just before the new school year starts. Maybe you're thinking: *But I have an app for that!* Or *It's already in the computer (or on my Facebook or in my email list or phone).* And I am sure you do. Please keep your favorite app. You need it to make calls while you are on the go or want to quickly recall the name of a parent in the checkout line at Target!

There may come a time in the very near future when everyone in every congregation will prefer accessing directory information digitally, instead of in printed form. I get it. But here's why we like getting a print-ready directory at the same time each year:

* One of the most chronic challenges to building a sustainable ministry is not having an updated database. We depend on the membership secretary and the church's software to manage our database for us. This almost never works.

* Having to come up with a directory that is print-ready forces us to pull the information we've got buried in a variety of places—in our personal address book, on Facebook, on a listserve, in our emails or our texts—and put them all in a single, accessible document with all the information updated annually. Unfortunately, it's normal for a children's ministry staff person to leave the church without leaving behind accurate contact information for children and families.

* If you're able to get a print-ready directory done for a couple years and you're ready to move it to entirely online, feel free. Let's walk before we run.

* There's a good chance that some of your volunteers will prefer having their list of students in print rather than online.

We've included a sample children's ministry directory in the online resources (ivpress.com/sustainable-children-s-ministry).

I know some people in children's ministry who resist tracking attendance. "It's not about numbers!" is a common refrain in most ministries. But we don't track attendance because the numbers are important, but because the kids are! Without tracking attendance, it is a near certainty that

* Kids will fall through the cracks.

* Your follow-up systems (whether for new or MIA families) will be hit or miss.

* Relational ministry will depend on a single point of failure (you) to remember who hasn't been around for a while.

* Your pastors will get inconsistent information about specific pastoral care needs for families with children.

Attendance tracking doesn't have to be complicated. Whether you use a high-tech database or a good old-fashioned spreadsheet, you can make attendance an automatic process by building your own attendance-tracking machine.

Whether you're using rosters in your classrooms or an electronic sign-in process, make sure that one person in each room owns the task of ensuring that attendance has been taken, that visitor information has been gathered and added to the list. Those rosters can be picked up at the end of each class and updated attendance information added into a master tracking spreadsheet. Depending on the size of your children's ministry, recording in the master tracking spreadsheet can be done in fifteen minutes or less each week.

Here's the piece that most busy children's ministry professionals forget: set a date on your calendar once a month to review the attendance reports. If you're using a large database program, don't get discouraged by the complexity of getting the kind of report you want. Keep asking and refining. Within a couple hours you'll have a reporting template that gives you a quick look at all the information you need.

Notice who hasn't attended in three weeks or more. Make a point to reach out to those families you haven't seen in a while. You never know what may be going on in a family and how much they might need the support, prayers, and gentle nudging of your call.

The easiest time to reengage a disengaged family is within the first few weeks of their absence. Your attendance tracking machine will help you reach out to them long before they have settled into a new normal of not coming at all.

The Visitor and MIA Follow-up Machine

In the last couple of years my family and I found ourselves looking for a new church home. It was eye-opening to be on the receiving end of a wide variety of expressions of "hospitality."

Frankly, I was surprised at how intimidating it is to visit a new church. I felt like everyone was staring at us. I really didn't want to stand out. I was afraid I would dress too fancy or too casual. I remember the mixed emotion of hoping that someone would notice that we were new—and being nervous that someone might notice that we were new!

Because we have children, I was particularly interested to see what I would find in each church's children's ministry. At one church, a member of the children's ministry staff walked me around their classrooms to see what was going on for kids. She made me feel so comfortable leaving my children for Sunday school. That personal touch was enough to ease my mommy mind and allow me to enjoy worship while my kids got to experience ministry just for them. We had a good experience at the church, but we never heard from the church again. And we never returned for a second visit.

At another church, we were greeted and directed to an information desk. A really friendly lady took down our information and explained a little bit about the children's ministry, including pickup procedures. I never realized how important it is for new parents to receive very clear instructions about how the pickup process works.

The kids enjoyed their time, but I still wasn't sold on the church. The next day, though, I received a friendly call from someone on the children's ministry staff. I never actually spoke with them. They just left a voicemail, thanking us for coming and offering to answer any questions. I was impressed. We hadn't made any other connections that day, but we went back.

It was on our second visit to the church that my husband and I saw something that compelled us to continue coming until we knew this was the church for us. Without the personal touch of that voicemail, I don't know if we would have gone back for the second visit. Both church experiences were good, but it was the follow-up that made the difference.

Please don't assume that a form letter from the pastor or a cute postcard from the children's ministry can be a substitute for the human touch of a real person calling (or even sending a personal email). You might even want to try a service like sendoutcards.com. It's quick and easy, and your teacher can turn a picture of a visitor's project into a card with a personal message. In addition to making the first phone call, you'll want your hospitality machine to include a tracking plan and to follow-up with all your visitors until they either become a regular part of your church or let you know they have joined somewhere else. Simply following up with a personal call or message on a regular basis will set your children's ministry apart from almost every other one.

Of course, your attendance tracking machine will be foundational to building your visitor and MIA follow-up machine. Keep a little folder in each classroom with rosters, a pen, preprinted address labels, stamps, and postcards. Each week, have your volunteers check the attendance, and if they notice that someone hasn't been there in a while, they can take an address label, stick it to the postcard, and write a quick note.

Safety and Security Machine

Though the average family with children will never see it, your safety and security policy may be the most important machine of your ministry. Since most insurance companies require their church clients to have some sort of child safety policy in place, most churches have one. But many of them are decades old and haven't been reviewed or shared with volunteers in years. If you don't know what your church's policy is, here's a process for building that machine.

1. Background checks are a good starting place. But they can also offer a false sense of security. For example, for every convicted sex offender, there are countless others who have never been convicted. Background checks only screen predators who have already been caught. And unfortunately, churches are often an easy target for predators.

2. Take a look at your policy and make sure it answers all of the following questions as a starting point:

   o Who is allowed to be with a child?

   o How many adults should be present in a classroom?

   o How and when should children go to the bathroom?

   o Who and how will diapers be changed?

   o How old do student leaders need to be, and how are they trained?

○ How do you handle children who come to church sick, and what are the measures you will use to determine when they are a threat to the health of other children?

○ How will you handle a stranger who is lingering in the children's area?

○ Which topics are off limits for discussion with children?

○ At what age is it no longer appropriate for a child to sit on an adult's lap?

○ Is it ever appropriate for a volunteer to have contact with a child outside of church, and what needs to be considered?

○ What things should a staff member or volunteer be aware of regarding posts on social media?

○ Which doors are unlocked during children's programming?

○ Are there any aspects of the configuration of your children's ministry space that require specific policies be in place?

○ Which volunteers will get background checks, and how often must those background checks be renewed?

○ What is the process of orienting all volunteers to safety and security policies of the children's ministry?

○ Who can a child be dismissed to?

○ At what age can children leave the class without a parent picking them up?

○ What are the emergency procedures if a child is lost?

○ If a child is presenting a danger to other children, what procedures should the teachers follow?

○ How can teachers be aware of food allergies to prevent introducing foods that can create an allergic reaction?

○ What should volunteers do when a child is injured?

○ How are accusations of abuse to be handled?

○ How and how often are toys and furniture in children's ministry rooms sanitized?

3. Craft some guidelines specific to your nursery. As an example, I've included a sample (see "Church Nursery Guidelines") in the online resources for this book (ivpress.com/sustainable-children -s-ministry).

4. Get your updated policy approved by the appropriate leadership in your church.

5. Add to your annual calendar the training of all your volunteers in the church's safety and security policies.

6. Review and update your safety and security policies and procedures annually.

The purpose of your child safety policy is threefold: the first is to protect *children*. When families trust us with their children, they expect us to return them healthy and unharmed. Many parents actually stay away from church when their children are little because they see the church nursery as a petri dish for childhood illnesses.

Second, your policy should be set up to protect your *volunteers*. This is why it is so important to train *all* of your volunteers on your policy. You should have something written in your policy that requires two adults to be present in each classroom. I can hear you saying, "Annette, I can't get enough volunteers as it is. How can you expect me to have *two* adult volunteers in every class?" You can't afford *not* to have two adults in each room. Unfortunately, there are children who will make up a story to get attention or hurt someone they are mad at. With two adults in a room, both are protected. Any suggestion of impropriety will carry very little weight if you have another adult present.

Third, your policy protects your *church*. When you have a solid child safety policy in place, your church is protected. When these policies are observed, your church can avoid incidents and scandals in the children's ministry. Just one incident occurring within a church can cause years of hurt for families, staff, and the surrounding community.

It is common for church people to assume they don't need to pay too much attention to their safety policy, because their church is like family and the kids are safe. However, this perspective is dangerous. Most offenders are not strangers, but are well known by their victims and families. That is why it is important that we hold *all* of our volunteers to the same standard.

Some volunteers may be offended and resist changes. But the safety of your children is a higher priority than not inconveniencing our volunteers. If someone refuses to comply with your policies, no matter how silly it seems, you're better off without that person in your ministry.

Even with a strong child safety policy in place, we'll want to make sure we have layers of protection for our children. We had a situation in my church recently that made a believer out of me.

We didn't know that a convicted sex offender was serving in our congregation. At the time, we only ran background checks on our children's and youth ministry volunteers. No one thought to check the ushers. Though they never interacted with the children, they did have access to all areas of the building, including the children's ministry area.

Isaac (not his real name), a convicted sex offender, had become a lead usher. He was a gentle and kind man. He didn't draw attention to himself but was respected by the whole congregation for his commitment to the church and his faithful service. During my tenure, Isaac ended up back in jail for offending another child. Though his offense happened away from the church, had we not had strong security measures in place he could have had access to the children at the church. We were shocked, saddened, and a little relieved for our church kids, because we knew that he consistently had to enter the children's ministry area to collect the children's offering.

Fortunately, we had worked diligently to ensure that it would be virtually impossible for a predator to have access to our children. By looking at each environment and asking, "Where could something bad happen?" we came up with several practices that made our children's area safer.

1. We always had someone walking the hall.

2. We greeted everyone, especially those who looked lost or we didn't recognize. (You can make great security look really friendly!)

3. We had a circular mirror installed in the corner so that we could see what was happening around the corner.

4. An adult *always* walked kids to the bathroom and stood outside the door making sure that the kids were safe.

No matter what your obstacles are, there are creative ways to address them so all of your children can be safe. Take the time to build your safety and security machine.

Check-in System Machine

A good check-in system can be a productive intersection between your database and safety and security policy. Regardless of the size of your church, you will need a plan for the following:

1. gathering information on visiting families

2. ensuring that only approved adults can pick up their children

3. contacting a parent in case of emergency (or for a fussy baby)

4. documenting the number of children in your care in case of emergency or evacuation

These can be addressed by your check-in and checkout system. Your system might be as simple as a sign-in sheet at the door of each classroom, with cell phone numbers to contact parents and a numbered sticker for parent and child, or it might be as complex as having sign-in kiosks, bar codes, printed name tags, and claim tags.

How do you know when it's time to upgrade to a more sophisticated system? That's easy. When the one you're using begins to slow things down to the point that parents are missing out on either Sunday school or worship. If it takes a family more than ten minutes to check in one child, it is time to modify your system. Modifying your system might be as simple as moving check-in from classrooms into a foyer or entryway so parents can sign in all of their kids at one time rather than individually at each class.

There's nothing wrong with handwritten name tags or attendance rosters, but electronically generated ones will always speed up your check-in process. So, if you are seeing long lines of frustrated parents, it is time to investigate some more technically advanced options. It's just one more way that we show our families that we care about them.

Facilities and Equipment Maintenance Machine

One of the most frustrating things a children's ministry volunteer can experience is to plan their lesson around a particular piece of video content only to discover that the technology in the room doesn't work. No matter how you feel about incorporating video into your ministry, I'm sure you can understand the panic that sets in when the equipment teachers are depending on lets them down. We worked hard to get those volunteers, so the last thing we want to do is to create frustration for them!

There are two simple things that you can do to avoid this situation. First, have a simple feedback form in each classroom. I've included a copy (see "Weekly Classroom Feedback Form") in our online resources (ivpress.com/sustainable-children-s-ministry).

Ask three or four questions to get feedback on the lesson, children, and equipment. Pick it up every Sunday after church, and look it over to learn how things went and whether there are toys or equipment that are broken or need attention before the coming week.

The second part of your facilities and equipment maintenance machine is to build a weekly check-in into your routine. Choose a day, and take ten minutes to check every piece of electronics. Turn things on and off. If something is broken, it is better to learn that on Thursday than Sunday morning.

At this point, if you're starting to feel overwhelmed, don't worry. It takes most churches months or even as much as a year to get all these simple "machines" in place. Give yourself plenty of time, and tackle them one by one. It may take you a couple of years to get some of these working the way you want them, but you will discover that each one of these machines—just like a lever or a pulley—will increase the leverage and magnify the impact of your ministry.

Seeing What Others Can't—Yet

Clarifying Your Vision

> *Given the seeming importance of retaining youth for most religious groups in the United States it is striking how haphazardly most congregations go about it.*
>
> TIM CLYDSDALE, *THE FIRST YEAR OUT*

I like to cook, and I'm just adventurous enough that I don't mind trying something new, even when I'm expecting company. The result can be absolutely amazing or a total disaster. I've experienced both!

I have tried recipes from old cookbooks, recipes handwritten by my grandmother, recipes found on the Internet, and those shared by friends. When I first started cooking, I would measure and remeasure, and then double check all the ingredients to be sure that I wasn't making a mistake.

I'm not as cautious now. Cooking now flows more naturally. But one nonnegotiable for me is a picture of the dish I'm preparing. I won't even start a recipe or even consider buying a cookbook that doesn't have a photo of *every* recipe, even if every single step is listed in detail.

Creating Visioning Documents

It's human nature to want to see what we are working toward before we start. A view of the finish line is critical for any sprinter. The cap and gown is an important picture for high school freshmen. A picture of our goal—even if it is merely mental—makes us all perform better.

If building our children's ministry were something we could do alone, we could hold a vague picture in our minds of our kids grown up, without their diaper bags, runny noses, and skinned knees. We could imagine them as growing, faith-filled teens stopping by to give us a hug the week they get their driver's licenses.

But regardless of our church's size or the number of kids in our ministries, we can *never* do this alone. And we need our team working with the same picture in mind.

For us, the picture comes in the form of carefully defined and clearly communicated visioning documents, including

1. a mission statement

2. measurable three-year goals

3. a statement of values

4. a ministry management chart

The mission statement. Many churches we work with can produce a mission statement (when prompted) for their children's ministry. Often that mission was drafted by one person sitting alone in their office, and almost no one (including the author) knows what it says.

Ministry Architects prefers to engage an invested group of parents, volunteers, and church leaders who will passionately wrestle to get the vision right. Because even if your sentence structure is sound and your word choice is perfect, without the buy-in of a team, your mission statement will typically lack the staying power needed to weather the to-be-expected changes of a dynamic ministry.

A simple Internet search will yield a wide variety of processes for creating a mission statement. For our purposes, though, there are three critical questions that your mission statement must answer.

1. What do we want to produce? Or, what is our impact? (Example: disciples, servants, good citizens)

2. How will we produce these results and create impact? (Example: through teaching, loving)

3. Who will be impacted through the ministry? (Examples: members, neighbors, all the little children of the world)

Once your team has wrestled with these questions and settled on the answers as a group, you can then focus on crafting a statement that clearly communicates who you are, who you are reaching, and what your ministry hopes to produce through all its efforts.

Once constructed, your mission statement should be communicated, celebrated, and referred to regularly as a touchstone. When I was leading a children's ministry, it was not uncommon for us to begin each of our staff meetings by reciting the mission statement in unison from memory.

If you regularly embed this language into your leadership meetings, the statement will become the measuring stick you use for assessing each program and event on your ministry calendar. As your ministry grows and changes, your mission statement will be a constant that ensures consistency and focus.

Your mission statement is a picture to keep in front of you and your team—some even hang it on the wall! The following are a couple of examples:

> The children's ministry of [name of church] exists to embrace, engage, and educate families of the church and community so the children will become lifelong followers of Christ.

> The children's ministry of [name of church] has fun, grows together, learns about God and faith, and makes the world a better place.

Three-year goals. Whoever said, "A goal is a dream with a deadline" was right. Our lives are driven by deadlines. So much so, in fact, that I challenge you to name a day in your last month without a deadline that directed at least some of your behavior.

Like a lot of people, I'd like to be healthier. The strategy for being "healthier" is not rocket science—drink more water, exercise, stop eating junk food. But *healthy* can be hard to measure. So I've tried to put a few specific deadlines to my dream of better health. I measure things such as calories consumed and calories burned, or servings of fruits and vegetables eaten.

Having talked about goals with lots of ministry people over the years, I know that you might be thinking, *Why does everything have to be measurable? Some things just can't be measured.* And you would be right.

Not *everything* is measurable, but if we want to make real—not just imaginary—progress, we need to measure a few things. In fact, of the four visioning documents outlined in this chapter, only one— three-year goals—is even remotely measurable.

Most churches want to foster lots of thriving, biblically literate, fun, compassionate little Christ-followers. It's a wonderful dream!

Remember, the difference between a dream and a goal is that a goal can be measured and comes with a deadline attached.

To get your wheels turning with goal setting for your children's ministry, the following are sample questions in different areas of your ministry that might lead you to setting specific measurable goals:

1. How many personal contacts would we like to make with parents of children this year?

2. How many nonparent, nonrotating volunteers would we like to have serving in our children's ministry?

3. How many children would we like to participate in a mission or service project in the coming year?

4. How many parent programs would we like to sponsor in the upcoming year, and how many different parents would we like to see participate?

5. How many children would we like to see assisting in worship leadership on an average week?

We recommend that every children's ministry draft three-year goals and one-year benchmarks. Here are a few guidelines that can help in that process:

1. Your three-year goals need to be enough of a stretch to feel inspiring, like they are too big to accomplish this week or even this year.

2. Your one-year benchmarks should feel like a significant, attainable step toward your goal.

3. At the end of each year, you will evaluate your progress toward reaching your one-year benchmarks and set new three-year goals and one-year benchmarks accordingly. (I've included a sample goals and benchmarks document in appendix B.)

4. Remember that your goals and benchmarks will give you the target but not the strategy for achieving them. Naming your goals and benchmarks gives your team a starting point for developing a series of game plans to beta test and iterate the process of achieving your goals.

Make no mistake. People *will* judge the effectiveness of your children's ministry by some standard. If you and your children's ministry team do not name the targets clearly, people will make up their own fuzzy and incorrect targets. Goal-setting allows you and your children's ministry leaders to determine exactly *how* the ministry will be evaluated.

And when a parent or an enthusiastic advice-giver approaches you with an idea for a new program, your goals will give you an objective filter for determining whether to pursue the new initiative. The ministry can be freed up from a pattern of stops and starts and unbridled distractions that so easily bottleneck your ministry (and your calendar!).

Your goals will likely turn out a little bit like my kitchen adventures. You'll experience absolutely amazing results and a few total flops. A mission statement and goals put a "recipe picture" right in front of you to help you keep the end in mind as you work the process of cooking up your ministry.

Values: guardians of the ministry. A set of written values protect the climate of our ministries. Here's what I mean: I used to work in a bank. We always had a security guard onsite. I never once saw any of the security officers stop anyone from doing anything. In fact, it looked like a pretty easy job. They wore their police officer uniform (all of them were off-duty police officers) and stood in a visible part of the building. Occasionally, they would take walks around the bank, making sure their presence was noticed, and then they would head back to their regular post.

No one ever talked about what they did for us. We just knew they were there and that they would share a laugh with us occasionally. Banks have learned that having a security guard present and visible is enough to deter the vast majority of undesirable events from happening. It took me a while to realize it, but now it's clear that our security guards' primary job at the bank was not to deal with bank robbers. Their presence created and reinforced a climate of safety for customers and employees alike, and deterred the behaviors the bank wished to prevent.

The values of your ministry work in the same way. Keep them visible and their very presence can protect your ministry from developing a negative or destructive culture. Sometimes we say that values define the spirit in which we accomplish our goals.

Here's another way to look at values from a more personal level. One of the goals my husband and I have for our children is that they get to school on time each morning. As a young person, I struggled with being punctual, and I really want my boys to be in the habit of waking up on time to get where they need to be without feeling rushed. I can't tell you how important it was for me to *make sure* they got to school on time.

Sometimes, in my passion to accomplish this goal, I spoke to my kids in ways that I would never want them to speak to me. I would start out gently enough. But eventually, after a few failed attempts I would find myself standing in the doorway of their bedroom, squawking, "Get up! You're never gonna make it on time! You've got to get out of bed, right this minute! Do *not* go back to sleep!"

In a saner moment (after realizing that my passionate commitment to punctuality wasn't working so well), I realized (repeatedly, I'm embarrassed to say) I was ignoring our values in an effort to achieve our goal. No one wants to start the day being screamed at. So I started to experiment.

I would head upstairs with a cell phone in hand cued with either a fun dance song or a funny YouTube video sure to make the boys laugh. More often than not, they would wake up laughing. The goal we wanted to accomplish—my boys getting out the door in plenty of time—was important, but not so important that it was worth violating the spirit we want for our family.

Sure, it's not always perfect. More easily than I'd like, I fall into old patterns that ignore our values. But the values are there to reorient me to the kind of family we'd like to be.

Values—like compassion and generosity, like playfulness and Christ-centeredness—guard the spirit of our ministries. Sometimes you may need to balance values that might appear to be contradictory. For example, the value of "fun" might look lazy and undisciplined, but adding a value like "responsibility" or "leaving places better than we found them" can help you strike the right balance with your values statement.

Keeping your ministry values in front of your parents, leaders, and kids can protect the kind of climate you'd love to see in your ministry. You can post them in classrooms, add them to your email signature or letterhead, or mention them in your volunteer trainings. As you post these "guardians of the ministry" as sentries throughout your ministry, you'll come much closer to ensuring that the spirit and culture of every program, event, and meeting consistently reflects these values. (I've included sample values statements for a children's ministry in appendix C.)

Organizational chart. The final visioning document you'll need is an organizational chart that defines who is responsible for which parts of the ministry, who connects with one another, and who picks up the slack if one person or group is unable to complete their responsibilities.

I know. You didn't go into ministry to sit in your office and draw organizational charts and define reporting structures and responsibilities. I get it. But if this piece doesn't get done, you'll wind up spending exponentially more hours doing things you like even less!

Let me explain. As we'll address in chapter eight, almost every children's ministry director I have known has struggled with delegating tasks to others on their team. If your structure is fuzzy enough that you have trouble drawing it on paper, it's much more likely that you'll stay trapped in the "workhorse syndrome" (see chap. 2) for a long time.

Writing down the structure generates accountability—both for you and for your team. When titles and responsibilities are mapped out, it soon becomes clear who is carrying too much and who could take on a little more. A good organizational chart is not a static document you create and revisit every five years or so. Reviewing it in black and white every quarter will automatically highlight the needs and opportunities for expanding your team or reassigning some of the larger load-bearing tasks of the ministry.

In Luke 14:28, Jesus warns us to count the cost when taking on a project. If you're like me, you would much rather jump into an exciting new initiative than stop to take stock of how the new initiative fits into the overall design of our ministry (and whether you can afford the time, money, and attention it will require).

We just might find ourselves managing our stress levels better if we matched each new idea with not only a new budget line but also an adjustment to our organizational chart. Like you, I *want* to say yes to great ideas. But I also know that not every good idea can feasibly happen today. Revisiting the organizational chart provides an excuse to push the pause button before saying the enthusiastic yes!

The unexpected happens in every church. There will be times when a decision gets handed down, and we have to paste together the resources to make a program or project happen. But even in this situation, you can check in with your organizational chart, count the cost, and make the changes necessary to get you through the roll out of the new project without a hernia!

In these unexpected situations (which are to be expected in any church), you may find the need to

1. ask for more help by perhaps hiring temporary staff, borrowing volunteers from a different pool, or gaining assistance from staff members outside of your department

2. suggest some modifications to the new program or event to increase the quality or reduce the urgency

3. consider scaling back current programs or initiatives to make room for taking on the new project

The time you spend working through the details building your organizational chart, including staff and volunteer roles, will pay you back many times over in time, not to mention provide peace and clarity. I've included two sample children's ministry organizational charts (see "Sample Organizational Chart 1" and "Sample Organizational Chart 2") in our online resources (ivpress.com/sustainable-children-s-ministry).

Once you've got your four visioning documents drafted, you'll want to take the time to gather feedback and input from an even wider spectrum of stakeholders—parents, staff, church leadership. It is not uncommon for the back-and-forth process of gathering input and redrafting the documents to go through multiple revisions and take a month or more. Don't get discouraged. This back and forth is all part of the process and what makes your vision stick.

If you find yourself needing help navigating the complexities of developing your visioning documents, we're here to help. Just email us at info@ministryarchitects.com.

Creating a Christian Formation Plan

Core competencies: hitting the bull's eye. Each fall, as my kids begin a new school year, I get invited to a curriculum meeting for parents. In that meeting, optimistic and energized teachers get a twinkle in their eyes as they review the core competencies of, for example, third-grade math. My eyes glaze over long before we get to multiplication tables.

But what these teachers are doing is important to their success as teachers and essential to my child's success as a third grader. Whether or not my third grader will be promoted to fourth grade entirely depends on whether he masters the core competencies identified for his particular year of school. Being clear about these core competencies aligns us all—parent, teacher, student, school— around the target we are all aiming for in the coming year.

Why is it, then, that when it comes to *Christian* education, we almost always fail to project desired ends for our children? We can do a lot to get kids in the door. (Have I mentioned how much I love bubble machines?) And we'll talk about these in chapter eleven. As sterile as it might sound to colorful, creative children's ministry leaders, we've got to "begin with the end in mind," to borrow Stephen Covey's wonderful phrase.

Most children's ministers will tell you that the main learning objective is some vague version of "teaching the kids about Jesus." But if we desire to hit the bull's eye of faith development in our ministry, we'll need to narrow our aim. "Teaching kids about Jesus" is a pretty wide target. However, I am sure that within that overall target, you can easily name a few more specifics. When we name and communicate our targets, our parents, children, volunteers, and church begin aiming at a clear bull's eye.

Here are the questions to ask: If a child is given the privilege of going through your children's ministry from birth to the end of their elementary years,

* What core concepts have they mastered?

* What core relationships have they formed?

* What core experiences have they had?

* What core practices are they now living out?

To break this process down a bit more, here are four questions to help you start naming your core competencies:

1. Core concepts: What does a graduate of our children's program know

   o about Jesus?

   o about themselves?

   o about others?

   o about the Bible?

2. Core relationships: Which people does a graduate of our children's program know?

   o leaders in the church

   o adults who have served in the children's ministry

   o peers

   o youth

   o younger children

   o those of a different race or socioeconomic background

3. Core practices: What does a graduate of our children's program do differently?

   o What are their daily habits?

   o What do they do in relation to the church?

   o What do they do in relation to others?

4. Core connections: What does a graduate of our children's program feel

   o about the church?

   o about God?

   o about themselves and others?

Putting it into practice. Coming up with your list of core competencies is no small task, but finalizing that list is only the beginning. You've merely identified the bull's eye. Next, we'll need to decide what tools and methods we will use to hit it. (I've put together a sample list of core competencies in appendix D.)

Step 1. Choose a curriculum resource (or resources). The most important tool you will use is your curriculum. You will want to choose something that fits most closely the culture and theology of your church. No curriculum is going to perfectly fit your context, space, and theology, but you will likely be able to find three or four that you feel comfortable with. Choosing a curriculum can be a daunting task, but once you have your list of core competencies, you have a measuring stick that will help you to evaluate different options.

A couple of other questions will help you to narrow your choices when it comes to choosing curriculum.

1. Do you want to use a curriculum with video elements, or would you rather avoid screens in your ministry?

2. Do you want something downloadable that you can edit before you give to your volunteers?

3. Do you want to follow a lectionary or church calendar?

If you have a children's ministry committee, you might want to get their input in this process, especially if some of them are teachers who will have to live with whatever curriculum option you choose. You may have one person evaluating for content and another looking at the activities, and maybe another comparing the curriculum to overall church culture. You might even think of other dimensions to evaluate curriculum by. When you enlist a group in this process, you gain buy-in for a final decision. If questions or concerns about the curriculum come up later, you know that the rightness or wrongness of this decision doesn't rest solely on you.

For tips that will help you begin choosing curriculum, see "Tips for Choosing Curriculum," included in our online resources (ivpress .com/sustainable-children-s-ministry).

Step 2. Set your calendar. Once you've chosen your curriculum, you can begin to schedule your lessons. What's nice about most published children's ministry curricula is that they are already loosely tied to the calendar. Most of the time, they are divided by quarter or season. This works great, because important seasons such as Christmas and Lent are already built into the schedule.

Most churches have a date for beginning Sunday school in the late summer or fall. It is great to celebrate kids starting a new grade in school and sometimes new Sunday school classes. That doesn't mean that you have to stop programming in the summer, although lots of churches modify their programming in some way over the summer. Timing the launch of your fall program with the launch of school makes sense.

Many families will have returned from vacation and are ready to reengage at church. Some sort of parent orientation or kick-off event in the fall can remind parents how the process works, alert them to any changes, let them know what you'll be teaching, and serve to articulate why being regularly involved can be so important for their children.

Once you have chosen your fall launch date, assign your first lesson to that date. Most of the time, you will be able to follow the lessons in the order they come to you from the curriculum. But there's a good chance there will be holidays and few unique events in your church or community that you'll need to work around. Scheduling your curriculum, week by week, at the beginning of the year will save you time later in the year, and you'll avoid that last-minute panic when your curriculum runs out and you don't have a plan for a particular week.

You might even want to color code your calendar, with each color representing a different item on your list of competencies. As you are planning your year, you will be able to clearly see what is being emphasized each week in each age group.

Step 3. Schedule milestones. Once you've chosen a curriculum that meets most of your core competencies and mapped it out on a calendar, it's time to schedule your milestone events. Milestones are once-in-a-lifetime celebration events that help children mark important points on their spiritual journey. Milestones have several defining characteristics:

1. They only happen once.

2. They are intergenerational events designed to affirm a child's identity in Christ and affirm their connection to the church.

3. There is a connection point for parents to be involved.

4. They include a ritual or tradition of some kind.

5. Usually a gift is given to the child, along with food to celebrate the milestone.

For most churches, baptism is a universally celebrated milestone. Whether your church is one who baptizes infants or baptizes later in faith development, baptism ordinarily meets all the criteria of a milestone.

The presentation of Bibles to children is another milestone most churches are familiar with. I love this milestone. It says to the child that they are ready to own their own Bible, reading to understand it for themselves. This milestone works best when children are recognized within the context of worship by their congregation as mature enough to begin reading the Bible on their own. Ordinarily, parents want to be present for this event.

You can see how this meets the criteria for a milestone:

1. *A one-time event.* Though the children may get many Bibles during their life, there is only one first-time Bible from their church family in recognition of their growing ability to know God for themselves.

2. *An intergenerational event that affirms a child's identity in Christ and their connection to the church.* The gathered congregation communicates to each child that he or she belongs in this community and that he or she is ready to take the next step in knowing and loving God.

3. *A connection point for parents.* Presenting the Bible in worship gives parents, even those outside the church, the chance to be reminded of and to embrace their own role in the faith formation of their children.

4. *A ritual or tradition.* Children traditionally have their names called, come to the front, and often receive a spoken blessing or prayer of some kind from the church's leadership. Perhaps a good example of this in the form of a yearly tradition would be a "Blessing of the Backpacks," which might happen before the start of each school year.

5. *A gift.* The Bible serves as a visible reminder of having reached the next step in their faith journey.

6. *Food.* Most churches have a reception following worship to celebrate and honor the children who have received their Bibles.

Many churches also offer a Bible 101 workshop for these children *and their parents.* This is a great time for parents to be involved with their children as they begin to own their faith and develop the habit of reading the Bible on their own.

Here are a few other milestones you might want to consider incorporating into your Christian formation plan:

* kindergarten graduation

* graduating from children's church and participating in worship

* rite of passage from children's ministry into youth group

I'm sure you can think of others. However, you don't want to have too many milestone events. The fewer you have, and the more you celebrate them, the more special they will be to the families of your church.

I know these power tools may feel a bit overwhelming—until you've gotten them in place. But hopefully, the step-by-step descriptions we've provided will give you the freedom to create and use these tools at your own pace. In the long run, the power tools will help you stay on a clear course toward your mission and get you ahead of the game in planning so you can focus on the *next* most important item on your list.

The Delegation Dance

Building Your Ministry Partners

> *How can you expect to get consistent*
> *results from an inconsistent process?*
>
> BRIAN SOUZA, *THE WEEKLY*
> *COACHING CONVERSATION*

> *80% of your problems are not people problems,*
> *they are system problems. . . . Your ministry*
> *is perfectly designed to get the results it's getting.*
>
> ANDY STANLEY, *SEVEN PRACTICES*
> *OF EFFECTIVE MINISTRY*

"So you work for the church. Full-time. I've always wondered: What do you do all day?"

I've sometimes had a difficult time answering that question. If you're a full-time children's director, you probably know what I mean.

"Well, let's see," I typically answer. "I edit curriculum, make shopping lists, get supplies, recruit volunteers, and send out lessons."

After thinking for a little while (and usually long after the questioner is gone), I think, "I update my rosters, plan advent activities, order third-grade Bibles, practice with the worship team." Before long, I can recall more than a hundred items from my task list. Knowing there are people who wonder what I do all day can easily make me hyperfocused on doing all the work myself, of playing the workhorse role until I'm ready to drop.

But it doesn't have to be this way. Ephesians 4:11-12 says, "The gifts he gave were that some would be apostles, some prophets, some evangelists, some pastors and teachers, to equip the saints for the work of ministry, for building up the body of Christ" (NRSV).

What would happen if we structured our ministry in a way that our primary job is not *doing* the work of ministry but equipping others to do it? If you're tempted to think this is a lazy approach, consider what might happen to a football team whose coach feels lazy for not dressing in pads and doing the same work as the players. Or worse, consider what happens to that team if the coach tried to play all the positions. The team wouldn't rack up many wins!

In children's ministry, we've normalized having one person *doing* the work rather than equipping and coordinating the work of others. But your team can be different.

Building a Children's Ministry Team

When I met Darcie, she was always in a hurry, rushing from one task to another, always with a frantic sense that there was too much to do. Every aspect of her ministry was under her close watch. She was managing an extraordinary number of details and almost nothing was falling through the cracks. Unfortunately, she was so frazzled that it often didn't take much for her frustration to bubble over with parents, volunteers, colleagues, and sometimes even the children themselves.

Because she was so hyperfocused on making sure that every detail of the children's ministry was running smoothly, she didn't realize how often she responded to parents and volunteers with a biting tone. She was the face of the children's ministry, but she was so overcapacity that she "didn't have time" to interact well with the parents, volunteers, and kids.

When I began coaching Darcie, I asked her to identify places where she felt stuck. There weren't that many, because she was so good at what she was doing. But she had trouble seeing the negative culture that had been created all around the children's ministry. In our monthly call, I asked what responsibilities she could give away. Knowing what you now know about the workhorse syndrome, you won't be surprised that she didn't want to give anything away.

No one, she thought, was going to get things done with the level of excellence and attention to detail that she brought to almost every item on her task list. And she was right. No one would. However, she forgot to ask whether anyone *should*.

Without knowing it, Darcie was taking care of secondary priorities (like choosing the right snacks at the grocery store) at a ridiculous level of excellence, and tending to first priorities (like caring for her volunteers) as if they hardly mattered. Jesus observed this same phenomenon in the Pharisees, "You strain out a gnat but swallow a camel" (Matthew 23:24).

Darcie was struggling with burnout, to get more volunteers, and to get along with key players within and outside her ministry. After a few months of identifying all the details of her ministry, Darcie began to see that she couldn't do it all herself. We came up with five areas of ministry and put together short job descriptions that clarified tasks involved in coordinating each area of her ministry.

Before long, she had recruited a hospitality coordinator who would make sure that new families were greeted and had received important information. Then a missions coordinator, a recruiting coordinator, a VBS coordinator, and a marketing coordinator joined the team. Darcie was more than apprehensive. After all, in her mind she had tried delegating before, and it "just never worked."

These five volunteers became Darcie's Children's Ministry Leadership Team. Not everyone played their role perfectly, of course. There were times when Darcie was tempted to take all the tasks back, because, truthfully, no one cared about the details as much as she did.

We had to talk her off the ledge more than once, helping her navigate the delicate dance of holding her volunteers accountable, but doing it with kindness, patience, and love. By the end of the year, Darcie had to admit that despite her lack of confidence in the process at the beginning, it was actually starting to work. These were real partners, carrying real weight in the ministry.

Darcie and her team found a rhythm, and she remarked that she didn't realize how lonely she had been, doing everything by herself. A self-proclaimed "hater of committees," she found herself looking forward to her team meetings once a month.

Darcie began to sleep better, spend more time with family, and feel that sense of accomplishment that had been lost in her busyness. Darcie, now close to retirement, sees an even brighter future for the children's ministry after she is gone.

God has brought you into your role and gifted you to lead your ministry. Your job is not to do *everything*, but to equip "the saints [that's your team] for the work of ministry" (Ephesians 4:12). As you think about building your team, I want to introduce you to the three roles that need to be filled to run a sustainable ministry.

The architect. The *architect* in your ministry serves a similar role to the architect on a construction project. The architect draws the plans and then makes sure the ministry is being built and executed according to an intentional design. Sadly, most churches work without an architect or any sort of overarching plan, assuming that they can build a multilayered, multistage children's ministry "on the fly."

In children's ministry, your architect would help you intentionally set the goals and mission of the ministry and make sure your programming is more than a conglomeration of creative ideas with no common ground, that all your activity aligns with your goals and mission. Without an architect, it becomes almost impossible to say no to any well-meaning church member with a new idea.

It should go without saying that just because an idea is good or creative, that doesn't mean the idea fits within your ministry's vision or goals. In our experience, one of the biggest reasons a ministry winds up being over capacity is because programs and events multiply without being anchored to a clear and compelling mission and goals.

The second responsibility of the architect is to keep an eye on what the ministry will require in the future. While others are taking care of the day-to-day tasks, someone has to be thinking a few years down the road.

If, for example, there is a demographic shift taking place in the community, how should that shift affect your ministry strategy? Or if the church is engaging in a new community outreach initiative, how will that priority affect the children's ministry?

The architect role can be filled by the director, a supervising pastor, or a layperson. But our experience is that these kinds of leaders are overwhelmed by the day-to-day whirlwind of ministry. Ministry Architects came into being out of this very need, allowing the staff and church leaders to manage the operation, while we play the architect role. (For more information about this, go to ministry architects.com/listen-design-and-build.)

The general contractor. The general contractor works in that space between *planning* the work and *doing* it. The general contractor makes sure each part of the building project takes place on time, with the right people doing the right things in the right order.

The contractor makes sure everyone on the team has been trained in their specific roles, has the tools they need, and accurately understands their specific jobs. Having a general contractor prevents having plans that are never implemented and ensures that ministries are not just busy and haphazard.

In children's ministry, this person might be seen on a Sunday morning going from classroom to classroom, making sure all the leaders are present, all the equipment is working, and all the supplies are where they need to be. During the week the general contractor makes sure all the systems are in good, working order (database, communication, hospitality) and the people assigned to the various roles in the ministry are completing their tasks well.

When, not if, things get off track, the general contractor encourages, corrects, supports, and troubleshoots problems. And though sometimes the contractor will need to jump in to cover a specific role in the ministry, more often than not, the contractor is recruiting a team and coordinating *their* work.

Typically, the point person for a children's ministry will serve as its general contractor. And sometimes a volunteer can be general contractor of a single area of the ministry. For example, VBS coordinator recruits, trains, and implements plans for an exciting week of VBS.

The skilled laborers. You can't build a house without people swinging hammers, pouring concrete, and installing an electrical system. If the whole construction team were architects and general contractors, there would be a lot of planning but little construction.

In children's ministry, without our laborers, lessons don't get taught, diapers don't get changed, songs don't get sung, and little cotton ball lambs don't get crafted! These are the hands-on people of your ministry. They are Sunday school teachers, greeters, check-in volunteers, nursery workers, baby holders, techies, singers, and nose wipers. Without these important people, ministry doesn't happen.

Some churches are filled with people who want to sit on committees and plan and talk, but are short on people who actually *do* the work. Other churches are filled with doers. But without the coordination and alignment that comes through a clear plan and a general contractor, these doers can scurry in a hundred different directions, often leaving chaos, hurt feelings, and discouragement in their wake.

When all three roles—architect, general contractor, and skilled laborers—work together as a team, children's ministry gets traction and leading them becomes a lot more fun.

The Three Works of Children's Ministry

Now that you understand the three roles, let's talk about the three different kinds of work every children's ministry needs to be doing.

Relationships. Faithful and effective ministry is always grounded in relationships—between leaders and children, between leaders, between kids, and between God and everyone involved. A healthy church fosters the faith of young people through faith-building relationships.

These relationships can look different at every stage. We nurture and build trust with *infants* as we comfort them, sing to them, and talk about God's love.

We introduce *preschoolers* to stories about God, but we are doing much more than disseminating information. We comfort, listen, and provide a space where safe and loving relationships can be formed.

We begin to guide *older children* beyond stories into concepts and principles that will shape their faith for the rest of their lives. In an ecosystem of caring relationships, we coach them, applying biblical principles to their lives.

These varied stages require people with varied gifts, and different children respond differently to different adults. As a

result, having a team of relational leaders is essential to a healthy children's ministry.

Tasks. One of the most surprising discoveries to people new to children's ministry is how many *tasks* need to be managed. If we were sitting together looking at your task list, I've got a good idea what that list looks like (and your facial expression as you're looking at that list!).

There are administrative tasks, scheduling tasks, communication tasks, designing tasks, accounting tasks, technology tasks, musical tasks, managerial tasks, spiritual tasks, marketing tasks, craft tasks, teaching tasks, cleaning tasks, organizational tasks, and tasks that sneak up on you and don't fit into any category. And in each category there are more subtasks screaming for attention.

Because you know about the workhorse syndrome, you know that our first inclination is to do every task ourselves. It's easy to be guided by the irrational thought *I have too much to do to ask anyone to help me!*

Building a great children's ministry team is never a seamless process. We set up a group to knock out a project together, and half of them forget the meeting or don't show up. We make a new policy about every teacher wiping down tables, taking out trash, and delivering lost and found items to the office each week, only to discover that in the first month only one volunteer is actually doing these tasks. We invite people to a meeting to support and encourage them, give them resources, and make their work easier, and only those who don't need our help show up!

As long as we are spending the majority of our time handling tasks that could easily be handled by volunteers, there is a good chance we'll feel like we're spinning our wheels more than we're making progress. I know that experience all too well.

In my first few years leading a children's ministry, I absolutely loved the energizing work of being in front of the kids, singing, teaching, watching them laugh, helping them pray. But working with database information on all my children and their families kept falling to the bottom of my list. I hated the thought of sitting at a desk and looking at spreadsheets for what felt like days on end.

As part of a quickly growing church, I found myself heavily involved with my current volunteers and families. With all the tasks I was doing, I hadn't made the time to meet new families or connect with prospective volunteers. I felt the need for more volunteers. I had asked everyone I knew, and I had exhausted all the personal connections. I began to think, *Why aren't there more people in our church who care about children?*

The truth is that there were plenty more, I just didn't know them yet. I knew the church had a database that kept the attendance of children and adults in our church. So I asked two dear friends—the highly organized kind who *loved* spreadsheets—to look through our attendance reports from the last six months and make a list of all the regular attenders, children and adults. This became my new list of volunteer prospects, which freed me to focus on what I was uniquely positioned to do—invite more people to serve on our volunteer team.

When I talk with children's pastors and I ask, "What are the things you wish you could quit doing?" I sometimes hear, "Nothing! I love it all!" And sometimes I hear a jumbled laundry list of tasks, some of which could be given away tomorrow but some of which are absolutely essential for the point leader to take care of.

The bottom line is that delegation can be confusing and complicated. It's not a single-step process. It's more like step, adjust, step, shift, step back, adjust—you get the idea. You'll be delighted to know that eventually you'll be able to use the filter *If it doesn't give me joy, I can give it away.*

Of course, there will always be some tasks you must hold on to as the leader, like recruiting, but there are many more you can (and should) delegate to someone who might enjoy that task more than you do. Usually, the things that give you joy are also the things you are naturally gifted at.

Some gifts and talents will be obvious to you, but others might require a little discernment or even an outside voice to bring them to light. StrengthsFinder (strengthsfinder.com) is a great tool for bringing your gifts, talents, and calling to light. It has been invaluable to me, helping me embrace the way I'm wired and helping me work with teams more effectively.

It will give you a boost to know your areas of strength, but until you've got your team in place and functioning well, there are going to be some tasks only you can do (and will very likely not get done if you don't do them). I usually begin with volunteer recruiting and training, building a database, and the annual ministry calendar. These may be items you'd like to avoid like the plague. But as you jump into delegating more intentionally, start by *not* delegating the tasks that only you should do right now.

Know this: there is someone in your congregation praying for a way to get involved or even just hoping to get connected to other people. Remember, you're not merely asking people to help you. You're inviting them to join in what God is doing in your church. You're inviting them into a circle of new friends that can become an extended Christian family to their children. Your invitation might be the answer to their prayers.

Events. The final kind of work you can delegate to members of your team is *events*. For better or for worse, events often become the only part of the children's ministry some people ever see. Events can provide a welcoming door into our church and into our ministry, as well as helping build community among the families who are already engaged. A well-executed event often gives us a doorway to punctuate the themes and spiritual principles of the year.

Early in my children's ministry career my supervisor would say, "Sunday and Wednesday are the most important thing we do." So, I focused all my energy on making Sundays and Wednesdays great experiences for children. But after a few missteps with major events, I realized the rest of the church may not notice if all the materials for each lesson are perfectly arranged in bins with instructions, supplies, and completed examples, but they *will* notice if our bounce houses aren't manned and ready when they bring their grandchildren to the fall festival.

The person who approves my budget requests is more likely to be at the Easter egg hunt than in the children's program on Sundays or Wednesday nights. So yes, while the weekly programs make the most impact, our special events are the public face of our ministry. Making those events excellent and engaging serves to amplify and expand the impact of our weekly programming.

It took me longer than I care to admit to realize that great children's ministry is not about choosing either weekly programming or special events to focus on. It needs to be both.

Linda thought that she had to be the one to manage every major children's ministry event. She would invite the same three friends to help. Then she would scramble for weeks, neglecting family, getting little sleep, trying to make every event epic. But with each event it was becoming clearer that it wasn't sustainable for her to keep using this approach. Eventually she began to entertain the possibility that someone in her church could manage event planning without becoming overwhelmed.

She began recruiting a major event coordinator for every special event in the children's ministry. (See "Volunteer Position Description: Major Event Coordinator" and "Creating a Major Event Notebook" for sample templates. These can be found in the online resources at ivpress.com/sustainable-children-s-ministry.) This person owns the event, but Linda regularly checks in on them and offers support every step along the way. Linda takes the time up front to equip the coordinator with expectations, contacts, and a rhythm of check-in meetings, and the coordinator carries the load of recruiting, ordering, setting up, and preparing so that the ministry can put on a stellar event.

The coordinator's focus on a single event allows me to keep my focus on all the other pieces of maintaining a healthy, sustainable ministry. I hope you see the commonality. In each of these areas of ministry—relationships, tasks, and events—God never intended for us to do them alone, at least not for very long.

Making It Work for You

Since there are so many skill sets required for a thriving children's ministry, the most successful ministries embrace the priority of building a team. Your team needs to be crystal clear on their roles and the mission of the ministry, but also free enough to work creatively to accomplish the ministry's stated goals.

I know that having a great team in place may seem like a pipe dream. You might hear the word *delegation* and think, *Yeah, great idea, but who exactly am I supposed to delegate to?*

The truth is that you can't delegate until you have a team, and building your team takes time and sustained effort. It's not impossible, though. We watch children's ministry people do it all the time.

Having a children's ministry leadership team is not something just for larger churches. *Every* church with children needs people willing to take responsibility for different areas of the ministry.

The problem with most leadership teams is that they can easily devolve into nothing more than idea generators. In the end, this group winds up giving you more things to add to *your* task list. You don't need a group of advisers; you need a group of partners. You need a team of people willing to roll up their sleeves and help do the work. Only then should you create a space for idea generation.

The following are a few of the coordinator roles that we've seen other children's ministries include on their team:

* hospitality
* recruiting
* supply
* music
* children's worship
* missions/service
* curriculum
* Sunday school
* midweek
* parent liaison
* class social events

In chapter nine, I'll walk you through a recruiting process to build the kind of team you're looking for. But first I want to offer a few recommendations for what you can do to keep your team inspired, aligned, and well-coordinated as you move forward.

Delegating, Not Dumping

There is a huge difference between effective delegating and just dumping responsibility on a new volunteer. When we dump tasks on volunteers, they naturally feel flustered, abandoned, and overwhelmed. And they likely will never want to volunteer again.

For example, I gave a supply coordinator a stack of lessons and asked her to get all the right supplies in all the right bins. I explained that I would be out all day and left her to it. I was disappointed with the results. Like I said, I'm a slow learner. I forgot a few essentials of delegation.

* One of the reasons people volunteer is for the connection with other people, often with the person who recruited them. Leaving my volunteer alone left her uninspired and missing out on the time with me she was hoping to have.

* I failed to give her enough details to succeed, and she left me with a huge pile of incomplete work.

* If I had made it a point to start the process with her and then check in every thirty minutes or so, the job would have gotten done (which would have saved me time), and my volunteer would have been excited to jump into another project in the future.

Delegating a task well means that we give necessary instructions and resources, communicate clear expectations and a deadline, and even then most volunteers will need ongoing support and trouble-shooting. In my example of failure, I could have provided a list of supplies for each class and given a list of what items go in which bins. And perhaps most importantly, I could have checked in throughout the duration of the project, providing a little encouragement, troubleshooting, or a vente latte.

Once your team has been equipped with all the information they need (which, despite our best efforts, is almost never *all* the information they need), the next step in delegation is to empower them.

Empowering Your Team

Empowering your team involves connecting them with the people and places they will need to know to successfully complete their role.

Let's go back to my supply coordinator. I needed to give her connections to the accounts and a tax-exempt card to use at local stores where she would be doing the shopping. I could have explained the process for reimbursement and given her the process for turning in receipts.

Instead, because I dumped on her, she had to come back to me multiple times with questions that could have been answered on the front end. Dumping rather than delegating wastes everyone's time and burns out volunteers faster than they can say, "I'll never say yes again!"

Managing Your Team

When your leadership team is equipped and empowered, you might think this task is finished. You would be wrong.

This is when your role changes from doer to manager. Instead of worrying about each item on a task list, you are finally free to do what you love—focusing your attention on the *people* performing the tasks while keeping an eye on the larger vision for the ministry.

On a practical note, because responsibilities of different leaders can vary greatly, it's hard to set a hard and fast rule for how often you check in with them. For example, the person who changes your bulletin board once a month may not need the same level of attention as your VBS coordinator. Here are a few rules of thumb:

* In the first six weeks, check in once a week.

* In the first six months, check in every couple weeks.

* After six months and when your volunteer is on a steady rhythm, fulfilling his or her role, you'll want to check in monthly for support, troubleshooting, and alignment.

Your check-ins can be a quick phone call or text, a lunch meeting, or talking in your office about how their tasks are going. The three key pieces of information you want to get from these interactions are

1. What is going well?

2. What is not going well?

3. What is confusing?

If you know these three things each month from each member of your team, you will be able to continue to empower and equip without getting bogged down in the details of each individual's role. If a problem is ignored for more than a month, it can affect morale and the spirit of your team.

Unless you ask, your team members may be tempted not to bother you, to keep the problems they are having to themselves. However, if you know they are feeling stuck, you can often resolve their challenge and make both of your lives less stressful in the long run.

Of course, one of the gifts of leading your team is that you naturally have the privilege of serving as a spiritual shepherd to them, not just as a manager. As you get to know them and talk about their lives, you will have the unique opportunity to pray with, encourage, and listen to them. But remember, you won't have the time or the energy to be *with* your team if you're trying to handle all the work yourself. Let's talk now about how to get your team in place.

Beyond Rotation

Building Your Dream Team

> *You do not have, because you do not ask.*
>
> JAMES 4:2

> *The army of God has a lot of demoralized leaders.*
>
> REGGIE MCNEAL, *THE PRESENT FUTURE*

I t's the Catch-22 of children's ministry. We long to provide consistent volunteers to create a safe, welcoming space for our kids. But if we overburden our volunteers by asking too much, we won't have any volunteers.

Is it possible both to provide consistent volunteers for our children and do so in a way that actually energizes rather than burdens our volunteers? I believe it is, and I will teach you how in this chapter.

If the single most common challenge children's ministries face today is a lack of consistent volunteers (and I'm pretty sure it is), then most children's ministry leaders are spending more of our time solving this problem than anything else, right? Sadly, no. We may be putting a lot of time into recruiting volunteers (for *this Sunday*!), but few of us are spending significant time trying to actually change the volunteer deficit in our ministries.

Few children's ministries tend to the *volunteer recruiting process* with anywhere near the investment it requires. So we accept the lack of volunteer support as normal, a fact of life we can do nothing to change.

Why do so many of us avoid spending time on the one problem that, if it were solved, would significantly lower our stress and multiply our ministry with kids? The following are a sampling of excuses (answers?) we've heard:

* Recruiting is hard.

* With fall festival coming up, I'm just too busy.

* Nobody in this church wants to help.

* The families in our community are overscheduled.

* We have a church full of consumers.

* Everyone is already burned out.

* I just got busy.

* This season [insert the nearest holiday] is so busy, it's not a good time to ask people.

Chances are you've been around the block long enough to know that blurbs in the church bulletin, passing around a sheet in adult Sunday school classes, and pastors begging for help from the pulpit don't work in any sustainable way. But most children's pastors are still looking for a quick and easy way to recruit volunteers, and when they can't find one, they simply give up.

Here's the bad news: there is no quick and easy way.

Here's the good news: there is a simple one.

Recruiting on Purpose

Most children's ministries have an intentional recruiting strategy. Most rely on the ask-the-same-people-in-the-same-way plan—a recipe for frustrated staff and burned-out volunteers.

At the same time, most children's ministers feel like they've done everything they know to do to get volunteers involved. Typically, I hear how hard the leader is trying to get volunteers, and yet each week the leader is scrambling at the last minute, desperately trying to fill the last few slots.

It's not that we aren't making the effort. But we are putting our effort into the wrong things. Sunday morning pleas from the pulpit or announcements in the bulletin might get us a little exposure, but shotgun announcements aren't the magic solution we expect.

One Sunday I was so excited because my pastor gave a great pitch for people to volunteer in children's ministry. It was *really* good! Twenty-eight people came to the back of the worship space and gave me their names and numbers! I was thrilled. My problem was solved, right?

Well, not exactly. After countless hours working through all the names, only two of them ended up on my volunteer roster. The rest were happy to bring juice and cookies every now and then or serve as subs "when you can't find anyone else," but only two were able to step into the roles I was looking to fill.

I was working hard, but in the end, it felt like I was wasting time getting lots of nos (from people who had signed up!). I found myself sporting a pretty bad attitude by the time I was through my list of twenty-eight "volunteers."

Announcements to everyone might be a step in the strategy, but one step is not a strategy. If you feel like you've been working hard and have done everything you know to do to fill your volunteer roster, you probably need a new strategy (or maybe a first strategy!).

Try the following strategy. Set aside a couple of hours a week to focus on recruiting. If this is one of your biggest challenges in ministry, you should be spending a chunk of time each week working on a solution. In all likelihood, you're already spending more than two hours a week scrambling to fill your volunteer positions week after week. And even if you're not, if you knew that you could solve your volunteer problem for many years to come, wouldn't it be worth the investment? Here's the plan.

1. Pray. Partner with the Holy Spirit by praying for the volunteer leaders you need, not simply that slots would be filled but that those who do serve would find themselves coming alive through their service.

2. Start early. Begin this process in February if you want a full roster of volunteers by August or September. The kind of people you want on your team are typically the kind of people who plan ahead, who are already confirming their fall commitments in the spring.

You want this kind of initiative taker on your team. Time after time, I've heard my colleagues in ministry say that the people in their church won't commit this far in advance. Some people won't, but many times the right people will.

When we wait until a month or so before we need people to start serving, those who plan ahead have often filled their calendars and their volunteer commitments to capacity, leaving you with people who make last minute decisions. These folks can be helpful in a pinch, but you can't build a sustainable children's ministry with them. Asking in advance communicates that the volunteer role you are seeking to fill is as important as serving on the PTA, as a Scout leader, or as a soccer coach (roles that almost always get nailed down three to five months ahead of time).

Sometimes, we think we can't begin recruiting in February because we won't know what we need until summer, because volunteers don't usually tell us what their fall plans are in February or March! February is a great time to check in with each team member, asking them how they feel about returning in the fall. There always are volunteers who are getting tired, and if we would give volunteers the option to say they don't plan to return, we will have six months to fill their positions.

More often than not, volunteers keep coming week after week, and no one knows that they are getting tired. They don't want to disappoint their friend, the children's director. But then the volunteer has had a difficult time in class one too many times and approaches the director saying something like, "I really hate to do this, but I just can't volunteer anymore. This will be my last Sunday."

Now you're stuck and only have one week to fill that vacancy. That's not fair to you, the kids, the other volunteers, or the church. I know it can be scary to ask volunteers if they plan to return for the coming year. They might say no! But it's a lot harder to learn that news at the last minute.

3. Identify your needs. This sounds so simple, but few children's ministry leaders actually develop a list of all of their volunteer needs for an entire year. There are many reasons we don't want to do this simple task.

* It's intimidating to look at a list of needs on paper. It's almost like getting on the scale and looking at the number. But in this case, it's probably more like getting on the scale on January 1, especially after you've enjoyed lots of holiday parties and dozens of chocolate Santas.

* We're afraid to ask for everything we need. When we write our list of needs, a sense of responsibility is attached to that list (and maybe even fear of failure). But if we don't ask, we know exactly what will happen: we'll "miss 100 percent of the shots we don't take" (thank you, Michael Jordan).

Your list of needs may include all the Sunday school teachers you need, how many people you need on your VBS planning team, special event coordinators, snack coordinators, a children's committee, and other volunteer roles unique to your church.

When you make your list and see how many volunteers you actually need, your anxiety might take over at first. The beauty of this process is that even if you don't fill all the positions (and *you will* if you work the plan), you'll be way better off than you were before. And if you keep working the plan, you will be encouraged that you'll never again have to feel this far behind in recruiting volunteers at your church. Once you've created your master list of needs, you're ready for the next step.

4. Make your prospect list. I hope you've noticed that you are at step 4 and haven't asked a single person to serve yet. This process helps us move beyond chasing parents down the hallway right before Sunday school, or asking your family members and best friends to fill in "just this once."

How many people do you need on your prospect list? Our general rule is that you'll need three times the number of unfilled positions on your needs list (step 3). So, for example, if you have twenty open positions on your needs list, you'll need to have a prospect list of sixty.

You may be laughing right now. You're thinking, *I only know a limited number of people, and they already are screening my calls!* How will you come up with three times as many prospective volunteers as you have open positions on your needs list?

The key is to tap into networks beyond your own! In step 4 you'll check with your pastor, your church staff, your current volunteers, and even some of the kids, asking, "Who in our church do you think would be great working with children?"

You'll scan the church directory for names. You'll scan the sanctuary for faces. You'll keep asking for suggestions until you get to your desired number of potential volunteers.

If you're like most children's ministry leaders we've met, you'll be tempted to shorten this process (or skip it all together) and start asking people to serve. Don't do it. Having this list—as hard as it may be to develop—is absolutely critical to the success of your recruiting efforts. Without it, there's a good chance you'll be in exactly the same place next year as you are today.

5. Merge your lists. Once you have completed your prospect list, it's time to decide which people you would like to see in which positions. Put one name in each of the slots on your needs list. Once you've got a name in each slot, you've identified your dream team.

The key is that you don't want to decide for anyone without asking them. Start with your first choice for each open position. Even if you think your favorite people will decline, always ask your "dream team" first. Even though you think they are too busy or won't be interested, give them the opportunity. You never know who the Holy Spirit might be stirring (especially if you've been praying)!

One more tip before you start the actual recruiting: ask each person to serve in a particular position rather than generally in "any area of the children's ministry that might fit best." If you ask and they aren't thrilled about the position you offered, you can always ask them to consider other options.

6. Make contact. For many of us in children's ministry, making contact is the hardest part. Once you've got your dream team list in front of you, I recommend you start by sending an email to *every person on your dream team list the first week*. Make your first message something personal but simple, and give them an easy way to decline if this is not a good time for them. (This will keep your message from sounding desperate.)

You shouldn't send a group email (e.g., "Dear wonderful potential volunteers") to multiple people at the same time. People who get those kinds of emails almost always assume someone else in that email thread will say yes. Group emails are simply too easy to ignore, and though they seem more efficient, they always take you much longer in the long run. In the first week, you may want to begin by contacting all your current volunteers to take the temperature of their willingness to serve in the same or a different capacity in the children's ministry in the coming year.

7. Keep contacting. Perhaps the most important step is to keep contacting. Each week, you will hear from a few people. Some will say yes. Some will say no. Others will say maybe. But the vast majority will not respond at all! Don't be surprised or disappointed by the lack of response. It is simply part of the process.

Once you've established your weekly contacting rhythm, you'll want to focus your two recruiting hours each week on making progress with every open position on your list, going back to your list of prospects, until your open positions are filled. Don't worry about finding just the right time to call or send a message. Just let them know why you're calling and that if you don't hear back in a few days, you'll try again. Most people will take their time responding to you, *even if* they intend to volunteer.

If you're playing catch up, this is going to be more work at first, because you're recruiting for this coming Sunday *and* next fall. But if you dedicate two hours each week to the priority of your long-term recruiting, you will never again suffer the type of volunteer deficit you currently have.

When Volunteers Rotate

Most children's ministries have settled into an uneasy and complicated rotation system with their volunteers. We don't want to wear out our volunteers, so instead of giving them a mission they can sink their teeth into, a calling that will actually change children's lives, we ask them to help out by filling a slot once a month.

Most of us have known (and some of us have been) people who have had a calling to children's ministry, who couldn't imagine not being with "their kids" every Sunday. It is these kinds of people you *huh !* want to build your children's ministry on.

When it comes to recruiting great volunteers, most of us start with this assumption: *Despite the fact that I think there is no more important ministry in the church than children's ministry, I'm pretty sure no one in our church would be willing to give more than an hour and a half or so a month. Maybe the committed folks would be willing to work with kids two Sundays a month. So I won't even ask anyone to serve every week.*

When we approach the recruiting process this way, we rob people of the chance to fall in love with children's ministry the way we have. So we always start by asking people to work with children on a weekly basis. Here's why:

* Our potential volunteers can always do less than weekly, but if we ask for once a month, there's not much chance they'll think we need them every week.

* People who help out once or twice a month tend to see themselves as helpers but not as partners who own the ministry to the children they lead.

* Children enjoy the consistency of having a few consistent faces to see every week, and they tend to be more nervous when teachers rotate in and out.

* A Little League team, a Scout troop, or Young Life club would never think of saying to their coaches and leaders, "Just come once a month, and we'll be fine." What we ask for speaks volumes about how important we think the role is.

* There are people in your church uniquely gifted to work with children, people whose hearts come alive in this work. Our greatest chance of identifying these folks is by giving them the chance to actually own a piece of the ministry, week in and week out.

Again, you're probably thinking, *I'll never get weekly volunteers in my church. It's just not possible.* If that is going through your mind, here's my challenge: this year, *ask* everyone to serve weekly. If they all say no, you'll have the joy of being right. If even one of them says yes, you're making progress!

Knowing that moving to a model of weekly volunteers may not happen in the first year or two of working the sustainable children's ministry process, I'm going to introduce a few volunteer-rotation models you can use during the years of moving your ministry to more consistent weekly volunteers.

Rotation Option 1: One Weekly, One Rotating

Just because not all your teachers can serve every week doesn't mean that you can't have one consistent, weekly teacher in every setting. There's a good chance you've already got a handful of volunteers who want to be with the kids every week. If you have six classes, you only need six people who are willing to serve weekly.

This person might serve as your lead teacher, but they don't have to be. You may find it more workable to have your rotating volunteer prepare the lesson each week and let your weekly volunteer serve as the master of ceremonies for the class and as the person who knows each kid's story a little better.

Some churches call that weekly, relational volunteer a shepherd; others call them assistant teachers. Regardless, it's nice to have that one familiar face, and whether they are leading the class or are more hands-on with the kids, everyone wins when you have this kind of consistency in your ministry.

Rotation Option 2: Every Other Week Teams

Another approach is to put together teams that serve together every other week. I know a church in Washington state that has an A team and a B team. The same people serve together every time they serve.

This arrangement makes scheduling easy for the staff, provides consistency for the volunteers, and gives the kids the predictability of steady leadership they can feel comfortable with. Even though they don't have the same teachers *every* week, children get to know two groups of leaders and have the blessing of twice as many godly adults in their lives.

Volunteers using this configuration find a rhythm of support with each other, especially on those days when the class is less than a homerun. And when a sub is needed, they have a natural resource to call on with the other team.

Rotation Option 3: Shorter, Consistent Commitments

We've seen some churches successfully ask for weekly commitments from volunteers, but for a shorter amount of time. One church does a workshop rotation model in five-week segments. Their volunteers commit for five weeks, and then have the option to come back the next five weeks or take a break and come back later. This also affords a level of consistency for the kids and allows volunteers who might not be able to commit for a year to make a meaningful commitments with a short time horizon.

Another church structures their rotation by asking volunteers to work every week for a month and then take a month or two off. Kids will get to know more adults this way, and it is easy for volunteers to commit to something they know they are able to complete.

Rotation Option 4: Combining Rotation Models

Some churches combine multiple rotation models. For example, if you hope to have one consistent teacher and one rotating helper, you might consider a shorter commitment for the consistent volunteer, say a semester rather than a whole year.

But whatever model you choose, strive for consistency across your ministry or you'll find yourself with a major headache on your hands. When you have one person who can commit to every six weeks and another who can commit to every four, and another who wants to work the second Sunday of the month, it creates more work for you and more confusion for your team. As the leader, you can decide on the model you want to use and ask your volunteers to commit to the rotation model that makes the most sense to your culture. It goes without saying: the worst rotation model is one that is filled in week by week, always at the last minute, leaving you reinventing the wheel every Saturday night. Period.

The Care and Feeding of Volunteers

Now that you've got a process for recruiting and scheduling your volunteers, it's time to build the process for keeping those volunteers engaged, trained, and enthusiastic about their work in the children's ministry. I know. You're thinking:

* I can't ask one more thing of these people. They've already done so much.

* If I ask them to come to another meeting, I might lose the few volunteers I have.

* These people have been doing this for years. They don't need any training.

I joined a new church about two years ago and quickly volunteered with the children's ministry. It was an eye-opening experience. For the first time in twenty years, I wasn't in charge. I didn't know where the extra scissors were kept, and didn't know if kids were allowed to go to the bathroom alone or not. I got a great lesson in how anxious a new volunteer can be. I volunteered because I wanted to help. I wanted to meet all the expectations. I just wasn't sure what those expectations were.

Certain things just shouldn't be left to chance (or interpretation). Things like discipline policies, ratios, bathroom and diaper-changing policies, and pickup procedures cannot be made up by new volunteers each week. These are important enough that everyone needs to be on the same page.

Thankfully, the staff took me through their onboarding process. Each week, a leader took me aside and went over five or six points of training, and as I learned the policies and expectations I became increasingly comfortable in my volunteer role. By the time I was finished with these meetings, I knew this was a church that would value my contribution because they had already invested so much time in me. I knew I wasn't just filling a slot.

The icing on the cake was a training meeting for all the children's ministry volunteers. The lead pastor started the session. It wasn't just his presence that got my attention (although that did say something about the importance of children's ministry in this church). When he said something like, "This is how we win in early childhood," he went on to explain the main objective with children of that age. He went on to describe a win with our elementary kids too. I was inspired—and relieved. In very simple terms, I knew how to be successful in my role as a children's ministry volunteer.

The same will happen for your volunteers. As they learn what success looks like, and they know which standard to measure their contribution by, their anxiety will lessen. And on top of that, they know when to celebrate!

Making Training Irresistible

Even though you might agree with me about the importance of volunteer training, you might be hesitant to put the training together yourself. In almost every church I visit, I hear the same responses about teacher training: "We have tried, and no one comes."

Let's make that reality our starting point. People are less and less likely to come to meetings anymore. If we know that's the case, you can still take responsibility (as the onboarding children's ministry staff did for me at my church) to meet with new volunteers one-on-one or in small groups.

Though not everyone will be able to come to the big meeting, you can still make sure they get all the information they need to launch well. A flexible coffee or lunch date with a volunteer or two can go a long way toward making sure your volunteers are getting clear directions and the necessary support as they step into their roles.

We know that most people don't want another meeting, but we can make sure the meetings we have are worth their time. Try these ideas and see if you don't have an easier time getting folks to come to your volunteer meetings next year!

Reframe it. No one looks forward to being talked at. But people love to be celebrated and to have fun. You don't have to call your get-together a "training" event (yawn). Send invitations, and make it feel like a party. My rule of thumb is this: everyone needs to be invited *three different ways* if you want them to come. A mass email just won't do it. The more personal your invitation, the better your chances of having a great turnout. I like to mail an invitation about three weeks out, send an email two weeks out, and make a personal call the week of my event. I know that takes some time, but the benefits you will reap from personally reaching out to your team are well worth it.

Create a culture of value. Everyone wants to be a part of something that matters. Make sure they leave your event inspired. Maybe a testimony (live or on video) from a young person, parent, or volunteer who has been blessed by the program. If all they receive from the gathering is information that could have been emailed to them, they didn't need to come to a meeting.

Make it fun. You don't need to talk that long to get your training done, so make the event into a party. Take the time to let your teachers build community. Use a fun game or activity as a part of training them in how to teach more effectively. At one event, we used a *Jeopardy!* game to teach our safety policies, and gave out play money for them to use to bid on donated items at the end of the night.

Respect their time. I know this is difficult, but if you want your volunteers to come back next time, start on time and end on time. It shows people that you value them and their time, and that you will keep your word.

Beyond the Victim

*Swimming in the Deep Waters
of Church Politics*

> *Leaders are responsible for both the big structures
> that serve as cornerstones of confidence, and for the
> human touches that shape a positive emotional
> climate to inspire and motivate people.*
>
> Rosabeth Moss Canter, *Confidence*

> *Speaking the truth in love, we must grow up in every
> way into him who is the head, into Christ.*
>
> Ephesians 4:15

As you have read through this book, you probably have said to yourself more than once, *But Annette! You don't understand my situation. The kids are great, but managing relationships with their parents and the church leadership is the hard part!*

I get it. Many things you are responsible for are out of your control. You don't always get to set your own event dates. Sometimes, a project or event gets dumped on your desk at the eleventh hour (like when your boss says, "You can do a little something for the kids during this all-church event this Sunday night, can't you? . . . With food? . . . For between twenty and two hundred?"). And even when you follow all the procedures perfectly, even when you get your event, music practice, or program scheduled exactly the right way, you can still get bumped by someone who "forgot" to follow the same procedures you were told to follow.

If you think there might be a story behind my attitude, there most certainly is! I was building a worship team for my elementary ministry, struggling mightily to put together some live worship music for the kids. After months of planning, cajoling, and recruiting, I found a drummer and a guitar player with a love for Jesus and for kids. I planned to fill in on the keyboard. But we needed to practice before Sunday morning. My new band members were busy people, and they were willing to sacrifice some personal time, each driving a good distance to come to practice. I found a time that worked for all of us, followed all the required protocols, reserved the room according to church policy, requested the appropriate media support, and invited my fellow musicians.

We were ready to prepare for leading our children in worship the next Sunday, the date the kids had been promised they would have a live band of their very own. But no sooner than had we gotten our equipment set up, young adults began flooding into our practice space. When I explained that we had the space reserved, the young adult pastor just smiled and walked down the hall.

A few minutes later, I received a call from the senior pastor's office asking me to give up the room. Of course, I should understand that since there would be more young adults coming, and because there were only three of us scheduled to practice, we should yield the space to the larger group.

I was frustrated and more than a little embarrassed. Of course, I gave up the space, and we ended up cancelling the practice. But I felt like I had let my team down. They had given up family time at my request. And I felt like my church had let me down. If you've ever felt this way, this chapter is for you.

Sore Loser

I *lost* the battle of the rehearsal space. For some reason the sting of "losing" at church hurt a lot more than I might have expected. I had the rug pulled out from under me by the very people who told me to stand on the rug in the first place! I'm sure the hurt was made more intense because I had such high expectations of how working in a church would and should feel. This was a far cry from what I expected.

I came out of that experience resolved that if the children's ministry was ever going to be all that it could be, it was up to me to make it happen. I couldn't count on anyone else on the church staff to take it up for me. The church had hired me to be the champion of the children's ministry. And if our kids were to get the kind of attention and priority they deserved and needed, it would be up to me. No number of unscheduled, uncalendared, interrupting, impolite young adult meetings could deter me from that singular mission. (Okay, I might have been a teensy bit bitter.)

I put my head down, doing everything I could to move the ministry forward. When people looked at me, I wanted them to see a hardworking, no-nonsense woman with a laser focus. I was on a singular mission, and I would not be distracted, especially by other programs of the church. So, there I was, me against the world, or at least me against the rest of the church staff.

Turns out, this may not have been the most productive strategy for building a thriving, sustainable children's ministry. By increasingly isolating myself from the rest of the church staff, I isolated myself from the rest of the church. Ours would be the best children's ministry ever, and—I'm embarrassed to say out loud—I didn't really care what happened to the rest of the church.

I would have been happy to see that rule-breaking, room-usurping, young adult staff person's ministry sink like a rock, forgetting that we were working in the same boat. My attitude was pretty stinky at that point. But somehow, this became the beginning point of discovering the road out of being a victim of church politics and into navigating this sometimes bumpy road with a joyful resilience and a healthy dose of humor.

A New Word for Politics

Few of us like the idea of playing politics, especially in our own congregations. It feels wrong and unspiritual for politics to *be* in the church in any way. We see politics as a way for people to broker power by being manipulative, underhanded, and divisive. In fact, one definition of politics carries this exact emphasis: "to deal with people in an opportunistic, manipulative, or devious way, as for job advancement."

Most of us have had the experience of feeling like the victim of someone else's manipulative techniques when we have felt taken advantage of for the sake of someone else's less than noble agenda. I don't want to minimize any of our experiences, but I would like to ask you to look at church politics from a slightly different angle.

Proverbs 21:2 says, "All deeds are right in the sight of the doer, but the LORD weighs the heart." It is easy, from our self-referential perspectives, to feel pretty good about the actions we're taking in the church. Our motives feel good and healthy to us. But only God can accurately evaluate our motives, and the motives of those we work alongside.

The next time you feel like someone in the church is being devious and manipulative, remember there's a good chance that the person merely wants to "get the job done" and probably even "bear fruit for God." And, if Proverbs is right and I can't accurately evaluate my own motives, I'm likely not going to do a very good job at guessing someone else's.

Dan Reiland writes in an article called "Church Politics,"

> It's rarely malice that drives the personal agenda. It's more often good people who really believe that what they are doing (what they want) is right. The problem is that good people who are attempting to do good things lose sight of the big picture and begin to justify their part of the mission as The Mission.

Instead of focusing on a word as loaded as *politics*, I want to suggest that we use a new word, one that feels more clearly consistent with values of the gospel: *relationships*. Before we can have politics in the church, we have to have relationships (good ones or unhealthy ones)— no relationships, no politics. If we took *politics* out of the conversation and replaced it with *relationships*, we would hear ourselves saying things like

* I don't get involved in *relationships* at church.

* *Relationships* have absolutely no place in the church.

* Church *relationships* can get really ugly.

* When it starts to get *relational*, I back away and take care of my own ministry.

Yes, relationships can be messy. But cutting ourselves off from others for the sake of "getting the job done" is worse. This kind of isolation leads to misguided assumptions, loneliness, and ironically *not* getting the job done. So how do we navigate the challenging, unpredictable waters of church relationships in a way that protects the health of our ministries, our churches, and our coworkers?

Making Relationships Count

When it comes to accomplishing the work of the ministry, the simplest tool we have is relationships. When I became laser focused on building our children's ministry, I began missing opportunities to build relationships with anyone outside our children's ministry.

As a young elementary coordinator at a large church, I started out energetic and passionate. It wasn't long, though, before I was buried under a mountain of tasks that threatened to consume my energy and passion.

I was stressed out. I was overwhelmed. And I consistently lacked the volunteer support our ministry needed. I barely was keeping all the plates spinning. I felt alone and clueless about how to build the ministry I knew the kids deserved.

I was sitting at my desk one day, completely spent, and knew I had to take a walk. I had a few things I needed to tell Jesus about this ministry he had gotten me into. This was *his* ministry after all. In my lament, I wondered if anyone else in the church really cared what happened with our kids. (Maybe you've been on the same walk.) Out of nowhere, I came to a slow realization. I didn't have a single friend I was spending time with outside of my children's ministry friends.

There was no one in any other area of the church I felt connected with enough to call on for support. I had been trying to get the job done, but in the process I had walled myself and my piece of the ministry off from the rest of the church. I had built my very own silo, and it wasn't working so well. And my teammates were drowning in the same deep water.

I realized that none of us likes to work with people who don't like to work with us. My hyper-ministry-focused isolation had communicated, without my even trying, that I didn't like and really didn't care about any ministry in the church but my own. In addition to my stance being less than faithful to the values of Jesus, it wasn't helping our children's ministry one bit.

I came back from my walk more clear than ever that it was time for me to step out of my isolation. It started out simply enough. I went out on a limb and actually *talked* to people in the copy room. I had always seen other people on the church staff as an interruption and distraction to my "real" work.

Then I took a big step and invited a coworker out for lunch. Eventually, I invited a few people to our home for dinner, with fear and trembling, knowing how limited my cooking skills were.

Ministry life was still very busy, so building relationships outside my tight, little children's ministry bubble took work. But after a few months, I actually had people on the church staff I called my friends. And though I am no longer on staff with this church, I am still close to most of those people today, genuine friends whose value goes far beyond having someone to speak up for me in budget negotiations or having a lunch buddy who will join me for sushi.

I love the way Gary Chapman describes the "love bank" in his book *The Five Love Languages.* In "relationship economics," our transactions with each other work not all that different from a bank account. The rules of deposits and withdrawals hold true in marriages, parent-child relationships, and friendships at every level.

When we invest in a friendship, our investment of time and effort gets deposited in our friend's love bank. The deposit may come in the form of giving encouragement, being a sounding board, or offering wisdom or a fresh perspective. But each positive exchange builds relational capital.

The opposite is true as well, of course. When we snub someone, ignore or dismiss them, we make a withdrawal from their love bank. I was blind to the reality that my isolationist habits were constantly making withdrawals. Do you ever wonder why the choir can get anything they want from the budget committee? Most likely it's because your choir director has built relationships well.

I had assumed that everyone else was playing politics while I was just doing my job. The truth is that I *was* playing politics. I was just playing very poorly. I realize now that every opportunity I had to partner with a coworker outside the children's ministry was not an interruption to my job. It was not just an opportunity to bless me with a life-giving friendship but an opportunity to expand the impact of our ministry as well.

Here are two important warnings. If we build friendships only as a way to further our agenda, we really are playing an ugly, self-centered kind of politics. At first, this was my approach. I set out to make friends because I thought it would help our ministry. I wanted to have friends who would make sure that children's ministry wasn't forgotten if I wasn't included in an important meeting. But when we treat people simply as a means to achieving our agenda (no matter how noble it is), we work at cross purposes with the heartbeat of the gospel.

Most relationships in the church will be with people who are relatively healthy and well-meaning, even if they disagree with us. If you stay in the church long enough though, there's a chance you may come across someone who exhibits what Scott Peck calls "malignant narcissism."

Not all relationships in the church are free of destructive intent, though fortunately most are. We would be naive to believe that if we try harder at relationships with colleagues, all will be sunshine and roses. Investing in relationships serves as a solid foundation for navigating church politics, but this step does not guarantee the way will always be easy or clear.

Adding Value

There is something else our imaginary choir director does we can learn a great deal from. They find ways to bring value to the church, not just the music department.

In most churches, music is a big deal and for good reason. When the music is good, the congregation relaxes just a little bit more. When something is off in the music department, you can be sure there will be drama. Since music is central to most worship services, your music director doesn't have to go out of the way to bring value to the entire church.

For children's ministers, the task of adding value beyond the children's ministry requires a little more work. It starts with deciding to be team players.

I know, none of us has time to take on yet another project. And if partnering with your church's youth department feels like a last-minute fire drill, then find other programs to support. But it's essential that we find ways to make a positive contribution to other people's ministries, not just our own. So get out your calendar and identify a few events this year where you and your team can lend support to someone else's ministry at a rate your team can handle with ease.

It could be as simple as being a cheerleader for the young adult ministry. If you have a resource that will help the older adults with their progressive dinner, share it. Over the summer, connect the youth director with your most helpful fifth-grade parents, knowing that most parents will allow their volunteer commitments to follow their children.

You can offer to have a few of your older elementary kids clean up after a women's ministry meeting (and then take those kids out for a little pizza or ice cream afterwards—everybody wins!). Adding value to other people's ministries doesn't have to require heroic amounts of time, just a little creativity.

Becoming a Children's Ministry Champion

You have probably noticed by now that the three steps I've identified in this chapter almost never show up in a children's ministry job description. All three of these steps, though, help to create an ecosystem of cooperation and ease in working in your unique ministry context.

The truth is that most children's ministries don't receive nearly the attention we might hope from the congregation and church leadership. As the point leader in your ministry, you have a choice: you can complain or you can elevate the profile of the children's ministry.

If you choose the second option, it's important to know that this approach is exactly what your church wants from you. As children's director, I never wanted to let a church staff meeting pass without celebrating something wonderful that had happened in the past week in the children's ministry or a child, parent, or volunteer who revealed the work of the Spirit.

Most weeks, when it was my turn to talk in staff meeting, with a wink I would say something like, "Since children's ministry *is* the most important department in the church . . ." One day, after making this kind of statement, my pastor asked me to stay after staff meeting for a minute. He said, "What you said today about children's ministry being the most important ministry in the church . . ." My heart sank. I knew I was in trouble. "Yes," I answered tentatively. He looked me in the eye and said, "Annette, I wouldn't want a children's director who felt any other way!" He smiled, I remembered to breathe, and we both went back to work, encouraged and grateful.

My pastor confirmed for me that one role I was hired for—which wasn't in my job description—was to be a champion and advocate for children, their families, and our children's ministry. In staff meeting, I recognized that everyone around the table was there to do the very same work for their ministries. I wanted to be careful to keep my comments light-hearted and fun. But I was making a point, and even on a bad day I got to promote the importance of children's ministry within my own church.

Many children's ministers feel like they shouldn't say these kinds of things. It feels like bragging. The sad news is that if you don't tell the good and miraculous news of what's happening in the children's ministry, most folks will never hear it. Sure, the youth director or the music minister may say something nice about what they observed in the children's ministry, but only you have the exposure to give a new story every week.

I never consider it bragging when I talk about the sacrificial effort of a volunteer, the tender pastoral needs of a parent with a child in the hospital, or the contagious love of Jesus in a six-year-old boy. If we want our children's ministries to be front and center for our church's leadership, we get to create the buzz simply by telling a great story once a week. Over the years of watching lots of great children's ministry workers, I've developed a list I call my "secret six"—six ways of we can add the championing of our children's ministries into the regular flow of what we do.

1. Celebrate successes. It's easy to get into the habit of completing an event, finishing a program, or wrapping up a meeting and moving as quickly as possible to the next thing. It doesn't take that much extra work to gather your team after each event for fifteen minutes, let them celebrate a few God-sightings, thank them, and pray for them and for the kids you've gotten to serve.

There is always something worth celebrating, if we're paying attention. You can celebrate with an email thanking your VBS volunteers or a bulletin announcement celebrating record attendance in Sunday school. Maybe once a year you'll want to go all out (say for the children's ministry appreciation dinner) and make a short celebration video. And once that event is over, you can share the video with the congregation on the church website. I love to interview kids and ask them questions about their teachers. The whole congregation enjoys this, and your whole church gets to share in celebrating your volunteers.

2. Share the bigger vision. Let people hear regularly what you are trying to accomplish in the children's ministry. You are not just filling slots with Sunday school teachers, you are asking people to stand in the gap to raise up a generation of lifelong disciples who will transform the world for Christ.

When you ask for help, share the big picture of where you want to go. If you are recruiting volunteers for a community event, go beyond asking someone to cook hot dogs. Make sure they know that they will be part of sharing the love of Jesus with your neighbors. Take that extra thirty seconds to help them understand the kingdom impact of the event and their part in it.

People have trouble being up on what they are not up on. When you share the vision, you help people understand a picture bigger than any individual snafu that may happen.

3. Embrace fun. If you're having fun, there's a much better chance the people around you will as well. When your ministry happens in a climate of joy and resilience, people are much more likely to jump onboard and give you the benefit of the doubt, even if they may not understand all the details.

I confess there was a time in my ministry when I felt like I was being criticized by everyone (usually for good reason) for letting so many details fall through the cracks. During this season I brought my defeated and cranky attitude to work with me every day. And— surprise—no one seemed to want to join what I was doing.

No one had the power to stop the cycle of negativity but me. I had to own the fact that being on edge and cranky was my responsibility and that, even when things weren't going smoothly, I had the freedom to find and embrace the joy and laughter in the work I got to do with children and their parents.

4. Share the dream. You have lots of plans and dreams for your children's ministry. Some of them have even made it to your calendar!

When someone asks, "How's the children's ministry?" skip right over "fine" and go right to "I'm really looking forward to . . ."

Paint the picture of a dream or an upcoming event with your volunteers, parents, and colleagues. You are giving the stakeholders in your ministry a way to think about what's coming. If you don't give them a good story, it will be easy for them to make up one that may be not so good.

Get your message to the congregation through pictures on the website, the newsletter, or on the screens in the hallways. Even if your plans aren't fully formed (when are they?), you can always ask for prayer as you finalize your plans.

5. *Build trust with key leaders.* Of course, in children's ministry, there are no unimportant "little people." But in every congregation there are people who have the trust of the rest of the congregation. When a difficult question comes up, the eyes of the congregation turn to those people for guidance.

As you celebrate your successes, share the bigger vision, and talk about plans for the future, give those trusted people a leg up by making sure they know everything essential about the work you are doing. This doesn't need to be anything formal, though there will be times when you'll want to specifically invite one of these trusted leaders to coffee to ask for a little advice and to give them a few stories to celebrate.

Your senior pastor should always have at least one recent story from the children's ministry to celebrate. If you greet an elder in the hallway, you can ask for prayer for your fifth graders about to move into middle school. And make sure your longtime members hear your missional heart as you share *why* you are doing a cookout for the community.

6. *Be patient.* Give yourself the time it takes to let change take root. Some organizational experts say that it typically takes three years for real culture change to happen in an organization.

Particularly if you are stepping into a ministry that has been struggling, give yourself the grace to let change happen at the Spirit's pace, not your own. As you bring change, you can be sure you will face resistance. Just bring your persistent, joyful, nonanxious leadership week in and week out, and the change will come.

You will feel like you are saying the same thing over and over, and you probably are. Eventually, the message will catch on, until one day, you'll start hearing others sharing the same vision you've been sharing all this time.

So, what if you decide that you just don't want to champion the children's ministry? What if you want to run the program and be left alone?

Well, get comfortable right where you are, because that's where you're going to stay. You'll be missing out on the momentum that comes from having colleagues, leaders and stakeholders passionately on your team, leaning in to help you make the changes that need to happen.

Once your message has caught on, you will begin to feel like you have an army of people to help when you've got a heavy load to carry. Without being its champion, your children's ministry may end up being the best kept secret in the church. Without a champion, the messaging surrounding your ministry is left to chance. Without being a champion, the wild winds of church politics will blow you over every time.

The good news is that we don't need to get wrapped around the axle of church politics. When we are prepared for the challenges and have laid the relational groundwork well, our efforts at change don't need to become stalled by nervous parents or anxious church leaders. We'll never get this dance perfect, but this chapter can be your beginning field guide to the secret world of church politics.

Children's Ministry Is Family Ministry

A Recipe for Turning Parents into Partners

It's hard to see the logo from inside the bottle.

ANONYMOUS

*Research in the sociology of religion suggests
that the most important social influence in shaping
young people's religious lives is the religious life
modeled and taught to them by their parents.*

CHRISTIAN SMITH AND MELINDA LUNDQUIST,
SOUL SEARCHING

It didn't take long to learn that children's ministry is about a whole lot more than children. Often, the first members of the family we meet are the parents. Usually, they're the ones bringing their kids to church, meeting the teachers, and evaluating our program to make sure their kids will be safe and happy during their time with us.

It's not until *after* parents have decided our ministries are a good place for their children that kids get asked that all-encompassing question, "Did you have a good time?" The answer to that one question can determine whether this family comes back.

Before we talk about the hows of partnering with parents, we have to acknowledge a challenge most churches face that stretches beyond creating programs and processes to keep parents in the church engaged and supported. First, we have to have the parents.

Here's what I mean. More and more churches are struggling to get and to keep families with children and youth involved. I often find myself sitting with pastors looking for ways to increase the number of families with children in the church.

Church leaders know that if they can't reach young families, their church is one generation from extinction. But even more importantly, we know that today's families, often minutes from our churches, are struggling like never before.

We know we have good news for them. We have a community of care and support for parents trying to hold their families together in a culture accelerating so quickly that much of what was nailed down is flying apart. In the midst of struggling, exhausted families in the blocks surrounding our churches, the most common question we hear is "How do we get them to come to church?"

How *Do* I Get More Kids?

You've probably heard this one before (maybe you've even said it): "Kids don't drive themselves to church." And it's true, they don't. As a result, our partnership with parents begins before those parents are even involved in our church, often before those parents even know our church exists. This is the crucial part of parent ministry that almost every children's ministry ignores.

If we're going to engage children who are not currently engaged in our ministries, that work begins by helping parents see the value in what we have to offer their children. Before they step in the door, we have to convince parents that doing so just might be worth the time and effort of getting their children to our program.

Attracting families not yet engaged involves more than providing a good program for those who come. The typical children's ministry professional spends almost *all* their time focused on the children and parents who already show up, and almost no energy working to engage more children and families.

In this chapter I will give you a number of recommendations for becoming a more outwardly focused children's ministry, one that consistently sees new families engage in the life of the church. But here's a secret: though my ideas might be brilliant, the key is not so much the ideas as it is giving persistent attention to reaching out to new families. Like so many aspects of ministry, the process usually works if we actually work the process.

There's no hard and fast rule, but I recommend you spend at least 20 percent of the time you allot to children's ministry in strategizing and reaching out to those not yet involved. A lower investment may produce some results, but you're not likely to see the sustained involvement of new families without spending a significant percentage of your time on this priority. Spend your 20 percent on these ideas as a starting point, and within six months you'll come up with ideas much better suited to your community.

1. Invite nearby families to events you're already doing. If you have events on your children's ministry calendar that usually draw a crowd, like VBS, an Easter egg hunt, or a fall festival, start there. You already know how to run these events. The piece you'll add is the connective tissue between your event and a specific focus on new families.

If your team is used to being event focused, don't be surprised if you get some resistance to inviting families from the neighborhood. We often hear short-sighted leaders—both staff and volunteers—

complain that parents drop off their kids for "free babysitting" or who come out of the woodwork for a fun event but never come back. This perspective misses the reality that these children and parents *are* the pool from which the new families—the ones you've been praying for—will come to your church.

An emphasis on engaging families not yet involved will require much more legwork, both on the front end and on the back end of your event, so you'll need three strong systems in place.

* *Promotion.* Your promotion begins with making sure all the information about your event is readily (and winsomely) available on your church's website. You can use that information for a flier, a postcard, or a poster to help promote your event throughout your neighborhood. A day or two before the event, it's always great to drop off a flier or postcard at one hundred or so houses in the neighborhood.

    If you've got a database of visitors with children, you'll want to send out at least *three* unique email invitations for them to join you. In addition, you can invite a group of active families in your church to each bring a friend or two to the event.

    The key to all these processes is persistence. During your first year of working deliberate promotion processes like these, you're likely to find one or two things that work well, along with a few that need to be adjusted. One key to a successful promotion effort is to focus on improving your processes after each event.

* *Contact information gathering.* Before the first new family arrives at your event, you'll want to make sure you've got a seamless way to gather their contact information. This step will allow you to invite them to future events and begin the process of letting them know of ways your ministry might support their families.

    Don't overlook how important this process is. Apart from the work of the Holy Spirit, nothing is more important to the process of engaging new families than building a database of parents and children who might one day become part of your ministry.

One of my favorite ways to gather contact information is to have some sort of raffle that gives away an item kids might value. You could have prizes for different ages, from a Big Wheel to a scooter to a bicycle. If budget is a concern, look for donations. The raffle doesn't have to cost anything at all. In order to have their names entered in the raffle, each family member fills out a slip of paper with the contact information they would like to share.

Similarly, families can "buy" limitless tickets for face painting, the bounce house, or the climbing wall by filling out a contact form. You may have to try a few different methods, but once you've found one, you'll finish every event with contact information for a number of families new to your church.

One final tip: for this process to work consistently, you'll need someone to serve as your VIP (visitor in process) specialist to update the database after each event and be in charge of regular communication with this group.

* *Follow-up.* After your event, the real work begins with adding all the new families into your VIP database. You don't want to bombard them with every email you send to your regularly participating families, so you should be strategic about what communications you'll send them, using this list as a starting point:

  o a "thank you for coming to our event" email that includes an invitation to "join us this Sunday for . . ." and information about who to call with questions

  o an invitation to special holiday events, such as the Christmas pageant, the Easter egg hunt, or Trunk or Treat

  o an invitation to be a part of any special rites of passage (e.g., Bibles for third graders) the church might be celebrating

- an invitation to any family-friendly events or mission projects

- an invitation to VBS, with clear information about how to sign up

2. Sponsor a program for the community. Another way to reach new families is to offer something of value to your community. Some churches offer a place for kids to come after school to have a snack and get help with homework. Others offer opportunities to play a sport or get some coaching at an incredibly reduced rate or free.

Basketball, martial arts, and even music lessons can draw kids that might not otherwise visit your church. We've seen many churches with programs like these—the most common is a preschool or a parents' day out—*but* there's absolutely no connection with or communication between the children's ministry and the families participating in those programs!

Have your VIP specialist ensure that your children's ministry captures the contact information for any participating parents or children who aren't already involved in the life of the church. At that point you can include these families in your deliberate follow-up communications.

3. Pleasant persistence. We never know when a family will be open to visiting our churches. So I am conservative about removing names from our VIP list. Of course, if someone asks to be removed from the list, we honor that request immediately.

Otherwise, we never know when a quarterly email or yearly phone call to a neighboring family might come at just the right time. We never know which families are going through a difficult season of grief or struggle. We'll never know if we never reach out. I know it's easy to see all this work as marketing, but once you have a divine appointment with just one overwhelmed parent asking for prayer, you'll never see this follow-up work the same again.

As long as you're giving something of value when you reach out to families, very few people will be annoyed (and many with thank you for the call). For example, if you are sending a quarterly email to families who attended your Easter egg hunt, attach an article or a link to a TED Talk they might find interesting, or a short tip sheet for parents. Always remember to include information about how they might comfortably connect with the regular life of the church when they are ready.

4. Stay connected with inactive families and children in your church. There is a good chance there are families in your church whose children are not participating in your program. This can be a hard pill to swallow. Often our knee-jerk reaction is to remove them from the children's ministry roles. But when we do, we miss a huge opportunity.

The good news is that these children and their parents already consider themselves part of your congregation, so you're halfway there! Sometimes they need the right opportunity to connect. I've seen too many of my children's ministry friends write off inactive children and families instead of working to connect them through a regular rhythm of reentry points.

* *One-off activities.* Like a pop-up small group, you can offer one-off opportunities for families to come together for something fun, like a visit to a park for a picnic or a group lunch after church for parents of upper-elementary kids or even a play group for younger children. When you make a personal invitation to MIA parents and children to these events, there's a good chance that one or two of them might show up, giving you the chance to learn more about their families and communicate the church's love and care for them.

* *Town hall meetings.* This is a good, nonthreatening way to get parents together so they can learn what the church offers for

their children. How about a father-child pizza party at the beginning of each year? We all eat pizza together, then we dismiss the children to the playground for twenty minutes while we share with the dads how important their partnership is, how they can help, and how our children's ministry can support their family.

Having an interesting discussion topic or a guest speaker can also be a good draw for parents, especially if there is something fun for their kids to be a part of during the program.

* *One-on-one meetings.* If families aren't flocking to us, we can always go to them. Invite a mom out for coffee, or invite the whole family to join you for lunch on Sunday.

Meeting with families will help you to learn what they need. When church families aren't involved, there is almost always a story much more nuanced than "they just don't care." We may learn that a simple tweak to the schedule could make a huge difference.

The time invested in getting to know our inactive families has great potential for impact far beyond your conversation. Parents talk to each other. If you've built relationships with a few key, inactive families and they feel like they've been heard, you will gain trust and loyalty, and they will bring others with them.

I've thrown a lot of ideas at you. You may be wondering, *What kind of results can I expect from these efforts?* There's nothing scientific about my estimates, but my rough guess is that maybe 5 percent of the new and inactive families you reach out to consistently over the course of a year will become involved in your church. This means that for every twenty new and inactive families you're working these processes with, you can expect that at least one will become regularly involved in the life of your church.

So if your church has a goal of engaging five new families this year, you'll need a VIP database of one hundred or so. And if you have a system in place you're working week in and week out, you may be able to do much better than this ratio.

What we know *doesn't* work is depending on the small number of visiting families who just show up to grow your children's ministry. This approach is what comes naturally, and it's the reason why most children's ministries are shrinking.

Focusing on consistently reaching out to parents and children who are not involved may require a significant shift for your team, as you invest 20 percent of your time in these initiatives. But if you'll give yourself at least a year of working these processes, you may just experience the fresh energy of new children and families being added to your church family on a much more regular basis.

A Recipe for Partnering with Parents

Kids who come to our Sunday school, kids' church, or midweek program are introduced to Jesus, who loves them, and they will be impacted by what they experience. But what happens when those children get home?

For too long children's ministries have functioned in a vacuum, focusing almost exclusively on the children. But how we relate to parents, grandparents, and other adult family members can make a huge difference on the effect our ministries have on the kids we work with. It has become a widely accepted fact that parents ordinarily have much more influence in the development of their children than the church does, which makes sense.

On Sunday, we can talk about life applications of the lessons we teach, but at home, children are actually practicing their faith (or not). At home they get to apply a lesson about trusting God when things don't make sense. At home they have the chance to practice love in an environment that might define love in different ways from the Bible. At home parents have the front-row seat in coaching their children (or not) through their wonderment and questions about God.

But not all families are the same, and different strategies we might offer will work with different parents in different ways. When it comes to parent ministry, one size does not fit all.

Not long ago, I recommended a meal-delivery service to my friend Erin. Here's how it works: the meal-delivery company sends a person a box with colorful recipe cards and perfectly portioned ingredients, allowing the person to prepare a balanced, delicious meal for their family without having to spend the time planning and shopping they normally would.

I love that someone else takes care of all the parts of dinner that I don't enjoy—especially *deciding* what we're going to eat! I have made things I never would have tried before. We have had lots of delicious dinners, and as our family prepares the meal together, we've gotten to spend more time working side by side. And so I recommended it to my friend.

Erin received her box of ingredients and instructions in the mail, and I couldn't wait to hear how much she loved it. When I called her, she said, much to my disappointment, "The food was good, but I really just don't enjoy cooking."

Hmm, I hadn't thought about that. But I get it. Some of the recipes take a little time to chop and prepare. It never occurred to me that the very process that relieved me would add stress to someone else who might rather just throw a couple chicken breasts on the grill and make a salad. While we both have the same end goal in mind—a healthy and delicious meal for our families—we came at that process from vastly different points of view. She values simplicity. I value the adventure of preparing something new.

Many books have been written about how parents can best support the faith formation of their children. And I'm afraid that many of them tend to assume that one size fits all families. My experience is just the opposite. A practice that is life giving for one family may be a real snoozer for another.

I wonder how our parents feel when we offer them take-home cards or links to videos to watch and discuss with their children. I wonder if they feel like Erin.

So as I offer a few basic recommendations for how to connect with and support parents, keep in mind that you'll eventually need a constellation of approaches, not just one. Now let me introduce you to a few of the basic components you'll want to include in your recipe for partnering with parents.

1. Provide the basics and beyond. The typical children's ministry partners with parents in two ways: take-home sheets and a periodic parent workshop. These two strategies are not a bad start, but they are just that—a start.

In addition to a wide variety of general parenting workshop options—both live and on video—you might want to consider offering a workshop or a six-week Sunday morning class just for first-time parents and those soon to be first-time parents. Our experience is that this group is receptive to changing the patterns of their home life and is motivated to do so. I have included a list of great parenting class resources in appendix E.

For many parents, though, the workshops we offer never seem to happen at a good time, and the take-home sheets never seem to make it out of the back seat of the car. And too often the families needing the most support are least likely to access these standard methods.

In the wild world of parenting—juggling jobs, kids, doctor's appointments, housekeeping, carpooling, and bill paying—are we delivering a box of ingredients they have no interest in preparing? I wonder how many families feel that what we are offering is arbitrary and disconnected.

Sure. Let's keep sending communications home with kids, and let's do an annual parenting workshop. But we just can't stop there.

Too many children's ministries assume most parents are just not that interested in the spiritual growth of their children. I don't believe it for a second.

Just because Erin didn't enjoy preparing a meal from a box, that doesn't mean she isn't interested or invested in the nutrition and health of her children. Knowing that countless families start coming to church when their kids are old enough to begin learning about God, we know there is a huge opportunity before us if we're willing to get a little creative in how we connect with parents. Based on what I see in the trash cans and in the parking lot, it may be time to bag the take-home sheets altogether!

2. Start a parent-connection plan. The best way I know to effectively support and partner with parents is to create the space (in our schedules and programming) to get to know each of the parents, grandparents, and others filling the parenting role for our kids.

Parents don't start influencing the faith of their kids because we give them a great discussion topic. Children are looking at their parents every day and learning how to be human in every way, including when it comes to faith. Parents are already partners with us in the faith formation of their children, and so there are few things more important to our children's ministries than building relationships with parents.

I know Sunday mornings are not the ideal time for you to have serious relationship-building time with parents. But your presence and availability to them during that time is key. If you are scrambling around looking for cotton balls, trying to get technology working, or teaching one of the kids classes yourself, you may miss your most important opportunity of the week—connecting with the people who have the most spiritual influence on the kids in your program.

While you don't have the capacity to immediately dive deep into relationship with twenty families, you can start with two. Maybe it's a phone call or a coffee date. Each week, you can connect with one new family in this way. When your parent connection plate is full, you might ask other parents to replicate what you have done with them. Before long, you've woven a web of relationships between a variety of parents in the church.

We have plans for almost everything else we do in ministry: curriculum plans, VBS plans, volunteer training plans, closet cleanout plans. Shouldn't we have a plan for something as important as building relationships with parents? You may feel like this is unnecessary or even arbitrary, but without a clearly defined plan you are destined to connect with a limited number of parents you already know well and are already engaged in your ministry. The ones who really need your time have yet to engage in the children's ministry. And, honestly, making this kind of plan can be pretty simple.

* Step 1. Decide how many families you want to contact each week or month.

* Step 2. Contact them.

If you have two or three questions for them, there's a good chance they will do the rest of the work for you. You could start with questions such as:

1. Is there anything I can pray about for you and your family?

2. Do you have any feedback for the programming offered to your kids?

3. Is there anything you want to tell me about your kids?

4. What do you hope for your child's faith development?

5. Do you have any questions or suggestions for me?

Remember, given the complexities of your schedule and parents' schedules, it may take three or four attempts to actually connect with a parent. Don't give up. Just build in calls to more families each week than you really expect to talk with.

After each call, make a few notes and include a date that you'd like to make the next contact. I've put together a sample Parent

Contact Tracking Sheet, which can be found in the online resources document (see ivpress.com/sustainable-children-s-ministry).

Whether or not the parent gives any evidence they are interested in the spiritual development of their children, you get the chance to plant the seed in your conversation. The cultivation of the seed in the meantime is up to the Holy Spirit.

3. Find the good and celebrate it. When you see the parent of a child in your ministry, and you have recently noticed *any* positive attribute in that child, make sure you tell the parent. Encourage your volunteers to find one good thing each week to tell parents about their child.

Even kids who struggle will give you *something* to brag about if you're looking for it. Things like singing, participating, laughing, being friendly, sharing, or engaging in the lesson are all expressions of something deeper being formed. And when children overhear us telling their parents encouraging stories, those children are much more likely to want to give us more of the same to talk about the next week.

We parents sometimes have trouble seeing the Spirit at work in our kids' lives, and we need a little help every now and then. I remember a conversation with Mark after my middle school son had come home from his first mission trip. I remarked that my son was a little disappointed that the mission trip wasn't more spiritual.

Mark and I talked a bit about how quirky and amazing middle school kids are, how sometimes they are like little children, and sometimes they behave more maturely than adults. I mentioned that after the summer mission trip, my son had begun doing his own laundry. I hadn't asked him to do it, he just saw that something needed to be done and had started taking care of it.

I didn't think too much of it. I just chalked it up to middle school weirdness. Mark said, "It's funny what we think spiritual is, isn't it?

Drew didn't think the trip was all that spiritual, but it changed his behavior at home. Sounds pretty spiritual to me."

Mark was right. Something had changed. It might have looked like laundry to me, but something had shifted inside my boy. And I totally missed it!

We can help parents begin to see the messy, transforming work of the Spirit in their children's lives simply by pointing out the glimpses of growth. We can help parents broaden their view of what is "spiritual" by pointing out what we see in the everyday behavior of their children.

When you see a child helping another child, be sure to mention it to the parents. Even if you don't have a chance to talk to them that day, you can send a quick email before you even leave the room. (I hear cell phones can do that these days!)

If you don't have direct interaction with most of the kids, make it a point to ask your volunteers what they see in the children they lead, and remind them to share those observations with parents. We all need good news every now and then, especially about our kids. You can make your church a place—sometimes the only place— where parents count on hearing something good about their kids.

4. Provide shared experiences. One thing that can get families talking faster than anything else is a shared experience. Think family game nights or family vacations that produce stories for years to come.

We can provide these kinds of experiences for our families through a wide variety of intergenerational family events. Some churches start by hosting family worship experiences. While this can be tricky to plan so everyone is participating, you can mix music that is comfortable for adults with a few songs that the kids already know.

Other churches do a great job with prayer stations during their family worship, which allow families to go through the stations together and having a different family member lead a prayer at each station. For most of us, praying in front of other people brings on a new level of anxiety. A well-designed debrief after everyone has experienced the same thing can provide a powerful point of connection.

Service projects provide another great way to bring families together. While it can be challenging to find appropriate work for the little ones, with a little creativity you should be able to find tasks appropriate for each age group.

If you're struggling to organize something for a larger group, you can always put together less complex service events involving three or four families. It will be easier for you to manage, and might just feel more comfortable for the ten to fifteen folks who participate.

A final idea is to take a program you've already got in place and simply add an intergenerational component to it. For example, some churches use the closing service of VBS as a great opportunity to bring in parents to be with their children. You may already give Bibles to third graders. How about adding in a reception with parents and kids following the presentation? If you've got a graduation or some other rite of passage from the children's ministry into the youth ministry, make sure you build in a chance for parents to be an integral part of that occasion.

Remember, you don't need to provide these kinds of experiences every week or even every month. A few times a year will be a great start to making "families together" just a natural part of the DNA of your ministry.

5. *Take it home.* So far I have talked about things we can do to support families and bring them together. The one piece I haven't mentioned is how parents can be more intentional at home about the faith formation of their children. Eventually, we would hope to see faith formation practices in the home becoming normal in the homes of children in your ministry. Here are a few ways you can encourage and strengthen these practices at home.

* *Holiday traditions.* If your families are new to the idea of developing faith-building practices at home, you might start with a holiday season such as Advent or Lent. Last Advent, my family set up a different kind of Advent calendar. We found a list of Advent words on the Building Faith website (buildfaith.org). Each day, someone was assigned a word and had to take a picture of something that expressed that word visually. We would share them with each other and talk about the meaning of the word.

* *Weekly verses.* We can pick out the fifty-two verses we would like children to know as a part of their spiritual background growing up, send one to parents each week, and ask them simply to read each week's verse during mealtimes. They can be successful in creating more spiritual conversations at home without making a new time commitment.

* *Spiritual vitamin jar.* As children step into a new phase of the ministry (preschool, for example), we can give each family a "spiritual vitamin jar" filled with verses, quotes, and stories on slips of paper. Children can draw a new vitamin and read it or have it read at each meal.

* *The family spiritual life plan.* We love asking our families at the beginning of each year to develop their own family spiritual life plan that answers three questions: (1) What do we want to do as a family to build our faith at home? (2) How do we want to serve together? (3) How would we like to be involved this year in the life of our church?

  I've included a list of great resources (appendix E) for parents to use as they seek to be more intentional about the faith formation of their children at home.

  Of course, the best time to start these practices is when children are little so they grow up with these practices as a normal part of their developmental landscape. As a result, first-time parents often have the greatest receptivity to these practices.

6. *Pray.* Pray for your families. As a leader in the children's ministry, you'll see and be sensitive to things that others may never see. Knowing how easy it is to underestimate the importance of prayer in our ministries, we can create a plan for praying for our families each day. Maybe you put each family's members' names on a 3 x 5 card and leave the stack of cards on a table, praying throughout any given day for the family whose card is on the top of the pile. Before long, you'll be praying for all your families in a regular rotation, without having to carve out a big block of time to do it.

We have the chance to turn parents into ministry partners by building relationships with them, meeting their needs, and exceeding their expectations. Perhaps like never before, busy, often-overwhelmed parents need the kind of support, encouragement, and good news that your church has to offer.

As you begin to build relationships with parents and families, be patient. With parents, we're playing the long game. The impact may not be felt in a week, a month, or maybe even a year. But as you work these processes over and over again, you and the families you serve will feel the impact.

More Than Planning

The Essential Systems of Chaos Management

> *Success is no longer related to the volume of tasks*
> *you complete but rather the Significance of them. As*
> *Peter Drucker once said, "There is nothing so useless as*
> *doing efficiently that which should not be done at all."*
>
> RORY VADEN, *PROCRASTINATE ON PURPOSE*

> *We're not saying that the whirlwind is bad. It isn't. It keeps*
> *your organization alive and you can't ignore it. If you ignore*
> *the urgent, it can kill you today. It's also true, however, that*
> *if you ignore the important, it can kill you tomorrow.*
>
> CHRIS MCCHESNEY, SEAN COVEY, AND JIM HULING,
> *THE FOUR DISCIPLINES OF EXECUTION*

Because we have so many different "jobs," it is easy for some of them to get ignored. And because the urgent things scream so loudly, we usually put off the most strategic, foundational things, at least until they become urgent! How many well-intended days have been hijacked by an unintended ministry surprise? The surprises caused me to abandon my plans for the day, which of course, only led to more things falling through the cracks.

Usually those surprises weren't really surprises. They were just tasks that had been overlooked so long that they eventually *became* urgent. Week after week, the cycle would continue. And week after week I would feel more buried under the weight of things I had to do *right now*!

So in this chapter I want to share with you a few hard-won tricks of the trade for managing the urgent while preparing for the future. Whether you're struggling like I was or you're an organizational savant, these tips might help you get enough altitude to tend to the things that matter most.

Balcony Time

In "the balcony," you take a step back from this week's or this month's tasks and look at the bigger picture of the ministry from a higher level. This is time for you to invest in the future of the ministry by strategizing, refining processes, and planning for the next few months or the next year. This is a time when you don't answer your phone or email, or work on this week's lessons or volunteers list. The result of your time will be clarity about not only where you want to go but which tasks deserve your attention this week and in what order. As I introduce you to the idea of balcony time, I want you to know two things.

* No single practice will affect the long-term impact of your ministry (and your own sanity) quite like making time each week for balcony time. When we look at our massive list of things to do, almost every task *spends* our time, while balcony time *invests* and *multiplies* it.

✻ Balcony time is so hard to build into most people's routine that it is practiced by only a fraction of people in ministry. Remember: if we want results that normal people don't get, we'll need to do things that normal people don't do.

Before you think balcony time is just one more thing to add to your task list, you need to know that we've never found anything that comes close to freeing us from urgency addiction and perpetually chasing our tails. Balcony time helps us tend first to the tasks that will have the most long-term impact while at the same time making sure that none of the urgent things gets dropped. If that promise sounds like a dream come true, keep reading.

Approximately 80 percent of your time should be spent on the operation of your ministry. We hear some time management experts tout the importance of taking time for strategic things as if strategic work should somehow replace operational work. Balcony time just makes operational work more productive and so much less unnerving.

That being said, it is mighty easy to get lost in the daily tasks that make ministry run. And as a result, most of us spend little time working *on* the ministry (focusing on the big picture and looking ahead), not just *in* it (the tasks of ministry). Working *in* the ministry involves 80 percent of your time—making Sundays happen, recruiting, and pulling off amazing events (also known as last-minute miracles). Working *on* our ministries—balcony time—helps us identify our top priorities and sequence them one at a time.

If balcony time sounds like a luxury you can't afford, think again. Avoiding balcony time because you're too busy is like not putting gas in your car's empty tank because you're in a hurry. If you want to stay in this ministry game for the long haul, it's absolutely essential.

Yes, it will feel like a sacrifice in the beginning. Yes, you will have to face the anxiety for a few hours when you leave the ground floor with tasks still undone. Trust me, those tasks aren't going anywhere. They'll be right where you left them when you step back from balcony time!

Balcony time is a high-yield investment instrument, but it can feel like starting a savings habit when you've been used to spending every penny every month. It might pinch a little at first.

Once you're in the rhythm, you'll want to spend four hours or so a week in balcony time if you're full-time. (If you are not full-time, try to get to about 10 percent of your work hours each week.) If you need to start with just an hour or less, do it. Here's a punch list I like to use during balcony time:

1. I start by reviewing all the roles in my life. (Balcony time is not just about thinking intentionally about your ministry; it's also thinking intentionally about your life.) The following are mine:

   o Christian

   o wife

   o mom

   o children's ministry worker

   o consultant

   o coach

   o writer

   o athlete

   o household manager

   o money manager

   o family member

   o friend

   For each role, I want to identify the most important task I can work on this week in that role. As a wife, it may be as simple as making sure that whenever my husband comes home, I stop what I'm doing and greet him. As a coach, I may want to order a book on coaching that's been recommended to me.

How many marriages fall apart because neither spouse take the time to deliberately improve their marriage? And the same could be said for our ministries. Tending to each of these roles every week means that at least once a week I'm doing more than reacting to what is coming at me in each of these roles.

2. Next, I review my calendar, looking ahead at least two weeks and looking back at least a week. This simple exercise prompts me to add more than a few tasks to my master task list.

3. Speaking of the master task list, it comes next. This is when I take time to update my master list of all the tasks I have pending. You may use an app for your task list or a legal pad or something in between, but the rule of thumb is that you only want *one* master list. During balcony time, you'll take all the stray Post-it Notes and reminders scribbled on your bulletin and drop them into a single list.

4. If you work this process for a month, you might be amazed by how many tasks make it onto your list. It's not unusual to have one hundred or more at any given time. But a list of one hundred is hardly actionable, and most of the time it's paralyzing. So the next step is to pull this week's tasks from your master list and put your master list away until next week's balcony time. We'll now call this your intentional procrastination list, since you will have given yourself permission to ignore it for the coming week (phew!).

5. Once you've got this week's task list in front of you, drop anything into the calendar that you need to put there. If you have a shifting sabbath day, this is the time to lock that day in for the coming week. This is also when you identify the times you'll be unplugged from work. Ordinarily, in addition to your sabbath

day, we recommend you carve out three additional slots (morning, afternoon, or evening) as off time.

If there are appointments you need to make or confirm, you can do it here. Warning: a calendar is for appointments (with yourself or someone else). If you're using your calendar as your task list, you'll be wasting too much time—like using a screwdriver as a hammer. We've all done it before, but it ain't smart.

6. Once you get all the urgent tasks under control, you can turn your attention to a big-picture project, such as

- your volunteer recruitment or training plan

- your one-year calendar

- making your database more nimble so you can more effectively reach out to new and MIA families

- updating one or more game plans, such as hospitality, parent ministry, communication, or rites of passage

- tending to your preventative maintenance calendar

- strategies for engaging more families

You may quickly discover, as I did, that as soon as you schedule your balcony time, the universe will conspire to interrupt you. You may decide that you'll need an extension office—like Starbucks or Panera—to give you more than five minutes of uninterrupted time in the balcony.

Rhythmic Week

In chapter eleven we talked about protecting personal time, not just for your own health and sanity but for the sake of the ministry. A weekly balcony time is a part of your rhythmic week, but now we've got to put the whole week together.

As I lay out my week, I like to start with naming my sabbath day. With the unpredictability of ministry, it's sometimes tough to have your sabbath on the same day every week, but it's good to have one set into your rhythmic week template to keep you from scheduling things seven days a week.

After you've blocked off your sabbath day, find a slot (morning, afternoon, or evening) for balcony time. Then you'll want to identify the program times that you're committed to each week (like Sunday mornings or Wednesday nights). You don't need to add all your meetings into your rhythmic week template. You just want your major blocks identified so you can have intentional rhythms of being fully *on* and fully *off*, and a few times that are somewhere in between. A rhythmic week for a full-time children's director may end up looking something like table 12.1.

Table 12.1. A sample rhythmic week for a full-time children's ministry director

	Sunday	Monday	Tuesday	Wednesday	Thursday	Friday	Saturday
Morning	Program	On	On	On	On	Balcony	Sabbath
Afternoon	Flex	On	On	On	On	Off	Sabbath
Evening	Flex	Flex	Off	Program	Flex	Off	Sabbath

We've already talked about all the slots except "On" and "Flex," so here's a little explanation for those two. "On" time is simple. This is when you are on task, handling the many operational tasks on this week's to-do list, including more than a few meetings, I'm sure.

The "Flex" time is a bit more nuanced. Flex slots are when you are off, but you are also available should you need to respond to emails or have a meeting. We consider these to be porous time off, fully interruptible. If you are taking care to protect your "off" and "sabbath" time, you won't feel taken advantage of when one of your flex slots gets spoken for each week.

One key: because our schedules can shift so much from week to week, the rhythmic week will almost never work until you take balcony time, and some of it is used to recalibrate your rhythmic week for the coming week. If, for example, you've been asked to speak at the church women's retreat on Friday night and Saturday, you'll need to move your sabbath to a different day.

If you find yourself saying, "I haven't had a day off in two months," it's likely because you haven't taken your balcony time and have chosen to play whack-a-mole with your task list rather than take responsibility for managing it. If your schedule is out of control, you're usually not a victim—you're a volunteer.

The Daily Six

In 1918, Charles Schwab was running a very successful steel company when he reached out to productivity consultant Ivy Lee. Lee said that he could increase Schwab's executives' productivity after spending only fifteen minutes with each executive. In that fifteen minutes, he explained his method to them. When Schwab asked him how much the consultations would cost, Lee said, "Nothing, unless it works."

After three months, Schwab wrote Lee a check for $25,000, the equivalent of $400,000 or so today. Here's his method:

1. At the end of the day, make a list of the six most important things to accomplish the next day.

2. Put them in the order of importance.

3. The next day, start with the first item, and only work on one item at a time.

4. If any items are left at the end of the day, put them on your list of six for the next day.

5. Do this every workday.

I wonder how much this single habit could transform the impact of ministries around the country. Try it, and I'll bet you'll discover that we all tend to put off the unpleasant tasks, even if they are the most important. It's easy for the most important tasks to get buried in a list of 30, 50, or 100 items on our list, and for us to ignore the steps that can have the most impact on our ministries.

I love the way my daily-six list forces me to make that difficult phone call or order new bulbs for the projector when I would much rather check my email (not answer it, mind you, just check it). I think you'll find a huge adrenaline boost after completing every challenging task, putting more wind in your sails for the next one.

Sunday Monkey Management

You walk down one hall on Sunday morning and the number of monkeys you collect can be astounding. Janet asks you to pray for her mom in the hospital, which you promise to do. Little Levi asks if you'll be calling to sing happy birthday to him on Tuesday, which, of course, you're thrilled to do. One of your teachers reminds you that all the ink is out of the markers for their whiteboard; you'll get right on it. The children's choir director asks you to announce the rehearsal time has shifted from 3:00 to 2:30 today, and asks you to distribute a flier to all the teachers. One of your volunteers who is going through a divorce asks if the two of you could get coffee this week.

Sound familiar? We call this challenge the fine art of monkey management. Every task that gets handed to you on a Sunday morning is another monkey climbing on your back. Here's how we define a "monkey" in this metaphor: a monkey is the responsibility to take the next step. Church hallways are an astounding place for monkey transfers. A person comes to church carrying the monkey (the responsibility to take the next step) and asks you to speak at Bible study next Tuesday. They ask, and instantly, the monkey jumps from their back to yours.

There is nothing sinister about this kind of monkey transfer, but if you're a monkey-management neophyte, the whole process can be a recipe for frustration and disappointment. Of course, you can carry a notepad (either paper or electronic) and jot down the monkeys as they come. You can integrate these into your task list on Monday morning. I've found this to be pretty difficult, so here's what I try to do: Unless the monkey giver is my boss, I ask the person to please send me an email or text reminding me. I say something like, "I love that idea! Could you send me a quick text or email about it? I want to make sure I don't forget in the flurry of the morning." I have communicated that what they have brought is important to me, so important, in fact, that I need their help to keep it in front of me. But I have left the monkey with them.

Preventative Maintenance Calendar

There are so many things to be tended to in the ongoing maintenance of a healthy children's ministry. Once a year, we need to do a thorough update of the database. Once a year, we need to revisit and revise our curriculum template and select curriculum resources for the upcoming year. Once a year, we need to update our hospitality plan, our attendance tracking system, our visitor and MIA follow-up plan.

A preventative maintenance calendar, just like you might use for your home (in April clean out the gutters, change the HVAC filters quarterly, etc.) helps your schedule when you tend to the larger, foundational components of your ministry. I've included a sample children's ministry preventative maintenance calendar in appendix F.

Once your preventative calendar is drafted, you can add those prompts into your regular calendar. If you're using an electronic calendar, you can set an annual reminder for the first day of the appropriate month to tend to that month's preventative maintenance tasks. If I know, for example, that I need to begin preparing for the Advent Fair two months ahead of time, I will set up a reminder on my calendar for October 1.

You can even add to your preventative maintenance calendar tasks that occur at regular intervals throughout the year, like checking attendance reports for MIA kids. In this case, you add "Run MIA attendance reports" to each month on the preventative maintenance calendar, then add it, say, to the first Tuesday of every month throughout the year.

These tasks are never urgent and, without this tool, often get overlooked, resulting in an increasingly unstable foundation for your entire ministry. Reviewing and updating your preventative maintenance calendar is a great task to add to your regular balcony time punch list.

Putting It into Practice

Every ministry is different, and each of us has different organizational tendencies—some, unlike me, are naturally organized, and others are not. Regardless of your natural bent, we are responsible for stewarding well the hours God has given us.

So before you turn the page to the next chapter, get out your journal (or phone) and write down three things you'd like to incorporate into your own organizational system. They can be things you've read in this chapter or something else you've wanted to try. But choose just three.

I'm easily excited, so I could see myself reading this chapter and wanting to jump into a complete organizational overhaul—tomorrow. Let's start with a few small changes that will stick, and build from there.

Give yourself a date about three months out to evaluate your new system. Go ahead and schedule that appointment with yourself in your calendar. If you feel like you're developing a good rhythm, continue what you are doing and add one new habit. If you don't, come back to this chapter and pick another idea or two to try until they become habits.

By now you've probably realized my conviction that trying to do multiple ministry projects at the same time seldom saves time. But we can do a different kind of multitasking—we can multiply the amount of work we get done by focusing deliberately on one identified priority at a time.

Your Ministry Marathon

*Preparing Yourself to
Go the Distance*

> *Above all else, guard your heart,
> for everything you do flows from it.*
>
> PROVERBS 4:23

> *Transformations come only as we go the long way round,
> only as we're willing to walk a different, longer, more
> arduous, more inward, more prayerful route.*
>
> SUE MONK KIDD, *WHEN THE HEART WAITS*

I was done. I mean really done. So done that I wasn't sure I even wanted to go back to church at all anymore.

After just two years of working in full-time ministry, I had endured all that I could. I started out confident and passionate. But after just two years, I felt like an ill-equipped, outnumbered failure.

The late nights, early mornings, and weekends away from family; difficult conversations; and criticisms left me feeling abused and accused. I had spent the last few months trying to convince myself that my current state of exhaustion and discouragement was part of fulfilling my calling of leading children to Jesus. But my strong will was writing checks my soul couldn't cash.

It's true there were things beyond my control that led me to step out of my first ministry much sooner than I anticipated. But now, many years down the road, I have to admit that the real responsibility for my emotional and spiritual (un)health rested solely with me.

I now realized that in the end no one else could monitor or protect me from the wear and tear of ministry. No one else could have told me when to say "when."

I hope I've caught you early enough. I hope that for you, saying "when" doesn't mean quitting but taking a deeper look at your emotional health and making the self-care changes you need to make before it's too late. Too many of us wait until we are spent before doing anything different. And once we get to that place, we may choose to get out of the game for good or sideline ourselves until our passion returns again.

Injury Prevention: It's So Much Easier

After working with hundreds of children's ministers over the past few years, I have now heard dozens of stories like mine. The names and the details may change, but the plot is always the same: a fresh, passionate, children's ministry worker launches and then leaves ministry broken and confused.

The good news (if there is any good news in my story of premature exhaustion and resignation) is that plenty of variables in my ministry were within my control. I know now that different choices on my part would have led to a healthier outcome.

The best comparison I can come up with is a sports analogy. Let's talk injury prevention. When an athlete is playing a sport, there is always the risk of injury. In the heat of competition, an athlete's adrenaline rush will push them beyond what they have done in their training. An athlete in top athletic condition has a body that can endure being pushed, but when a body hasn't been properly conditioned, pushing too hard almost always results in an injury.

My husband plays on a recreational soccer team. They only play one game on the weekend. There are no practices. There is no coach telling them what kind of workouts they should do during the week. Some of the players have a good workout routine on their own, but others are swallowed up by the daily grind of work and family responsibilities. For some players, the once-a-week, Sunday afternoon game is their only athletic outlet all week.

They really look forward to their games. It's a great way to blow off steam, see friends, and get a little exercise. The downside is how many of the players get injured and how frequently they are sidelined by those injuries. By contrast, the few players who have tended to their own conditioning pop up from a fall like nothing happened and get right back in the game.

I hope you're already seeing the connection to ministry. Once we step into a leadership position in ministry, we often lose our "spiritual trainer," who has kept us in good emotional and spiritual shape. When our trainer (our pastor) becomes our boss, something shifts. And often, without realizing it, we are on our own to fall into the bad habits of urgency and lousy self-care.

Without an intentional coach or mentor, we can easily find ourselves becoming a lot like casual weekend soccer players. We play hard, giving it everything we've got, not even thinking about the possibility of an injury.

It is the rare church that assigns a mentor or hires a coach for their children's ministry director. If that is something you don't already have, you owe it to your ministry to seek one out.

Whether in athletics or life or ministry, your coach will tell you that your daily practices determine your overall success. When a hundred priorities fly at us every week, it can be difficult to carve out time for tasks that don't yield immediate results. But without a stubborn attention to little, daily habits, our souls are ripe for injury and burnout.

I experience seasons when I'm more awake to the things of God, when I seem to be able to see traces of God in every segment of my life. And then, boom, a time of incredible spiritual dryness comes, as if out of nowhere.

When I hit those desert times, I let my busyness and being overwhelmed set my priorities. And like Peter, who, after taking a few amazing steps on the water, couldn't keep his eyes off of the urgent, tumbling waves around him, I start to sink. The little habits keeping me emotionally and spiritually healthy fly out the window, and I let the churn of my surroundings define the state of my soul. Maybe you can relate.

If you're in a healthy place emotionally and spiritually today, it's a good time to take inventory of your regular practices. If you're in an unhealthy place, it's an even better time.

Write your answers to the following, and refer to them every couple of months to make sure you are still conditioning your soul. If you are in a healthy place, the answers to these questions will become your spiritual/emotional preventative maintenance plan.

1. What rhythm of prayer and time in Scripture do I need for my soul to stay alive and healthy? Am I getting the time I need?

2. How often do I need to worship with others? (Sitting in the early service while you're planning your children's message doesn't exactly count.) Am I giving myself the time to be alive and attentive in worship with others?

3. Do I have life-giving relationships outside of my church? How often do I need to interact with these people? Am I getting the time I need?

4. Am I taking a twenty-four-hour sabbath from ministry each week (not answering emails, texts, or phone calls regarding the ministry)?

5. When do I take the time to work *on plans* for my life and ministry, and not just the tasks at hand?

6. What do I do for fun (hobbies, sports, creative projects, reading, etc.)? And how often?

7. What kind of rest do I need? What kind of rest am I getting?

Based on your answers, how would you describe the state of your emotional and spiritual health these days? As you look at your rhythm of self-care (or lack thereof), do you see any warning lights on the dashboard of your soul? Just to keep things interesting and to create a little sense of accountability, share the results of this inventory with someone you trust, and open yourself to their input.

Proverbs 4:23 says, "Above all else, guard your heart." Taking time to tend to your soul is not an elective course for people in ministry. It is a prerequisite for everything else you'll be trying to do.

Paying Attention to Warning Lights

There comes a point, for some of us, when it might be too late for prevention. It happened to me. I thought I was coping, when in fact I was spiraling out of control. I was depressed, sleep deprived, and consistently on the edge of my next emotional outburst. I was running on urgency adrenaline and caffeine most of the time.

There were warning signs along the way. I just refused to pay attention. I took on too many little tasks ("Oh, I can take care of that"; "Sure, let me take that one"), imagining a mystical future when I would magically have time to get everything done. I was sure I was strong enough to power through.

The cause was so important. It was worth the cost. I would put my head down and never, never, *never* give up. To an outsider, I might have appeared to be full of faith and hope for the ministry, but on the inside I was crumbling. The only problem was that I didn't know it. Jeremiah was right when he said, "The heart is deceitful above all things" (Jeremiah 19:9 NKJV). I became the victim of my own deceptive heart.

God has wired us with coping mechanisms designed to help us cope with short-term stress. It's amazing the ability we have to power through when the situation calls for it. We can skip sleep once in a while, but after months of living sleep deprived on adrenaline, what was meant to help us over a hump can become an ongoing lifestyle, a self-destructive lifestyle.

My favorite defense mechanism is denial. If given a choice between blaming, projection, passive-aggressive behavior, or any of those other defense mechanisms we learned in Psychology 101, I will choose denial every time. Over the years, I have perfected my denial skills. I'm like a denial ninja.

I believed that I was showing the love of Christ and being mature enough to forgive. Really, I was ignoring my heart and my body's warning signs, absolutely confident that the best way to deal with my sense of failure and hurt was to ignore it.

I felt rejected and criticized, overworked and underappreciated. And rather than deal with those realities, I kept my game face on and powered through the next big event with as much passion and flair as I could muster.

My denial disguised itself as forgiveness. It might have been more appropriately called *faux*giveness. Though I *had* chosen to forgive those who had wounded me, it was fake forgiveness until I had dealt with the depth of my own coming apart. The Band-aid on the wound was just not big enough to cover the growing infection, and some ugly things were happening in my soul.

It's as if I believed it would be weak and unspiritual to acknowledge that I was not in an emotionally healthy place. So I put on my best "Christian" face and redoubled my efforts to try harder to serve God.

Though I had prayed (oh, had I prayed!), I wasn't praying the honest laments that fill the psalms as much as I was somehow trying to protect Jesus' reputation (crazy, I know). I mean, if the gospel really is good news, and I am its representative, Jesus *needs* me to get my act together. The lives of so many kids depend on it. Not that any of these thoughts were conscious to me at the time, but looking back, this seems to be the narrative I was telling myself.

Eventually, something had to give. The day I realized I could no longer trust myself is the day I began to find my freedom.

Though I could have qualified as a card-carrying member of the Walking Wounded Club, I didn't know it. I missed the signs. They were there all along, but I couldn't see them. I thought I had the whole situation under control.

Warning Sign 1: Concerned Friends and Family

Though I wasn't seeking clarity or perspective from a coach, a counselor, or a mentor, I was fortunate enough to have family members who saw what I couldn't see. They raised questions about my health. They observed that I seemed to have lost my appetite for fun or that I wasn't getting enough sleep.

In my state of self-deception, I thought that those things made me a better Christian and a better children's minister. Even though I didn't know *what* I was supposed to do to change, I could have taken this warning sign as an invitation to finally ask for help—not for the ministry but for me.

Warning Sign 2: The Martyr Complex

I'm sure my responses to my concerned friends and family sounded more than a little condescending and self-righteous. Yes, I *was* sacrificing my own life for the sake of the ministry. It's what ministry is all about. I knew it would be hard when I started.

The crazy thing is that despite throwing myself at my work with selfless abandon, I wasn't receiving any accolades or earning any medals from my colleagues or the church's leadership. No problem. After all, I perform for an Audience of One anyway.

I thought my busyness and exhaustion made me better than the rest of my friends, but no one seemed to be impressed (which only made me want to sacrifice more). When we give up the things we need to do this work—like sleep or sabbath or a life outside of ministry—for the sake of the work, it never works out.

Warning Sign 3: Personality Changes

By nature, I am pretty easygoing, but you sure wouldn't have known it in this season of my life. Ordinarily it takes quite a bit to get me upset or angry, but all that changed—drastically.

Something as simple as a finicky copy machine could send me over the edge. I'm too embarrassed to tell about the times I lost my temper with volunteers and parents. For the most part I was professional enough, but every now and then I could see their faces drop as my tone became biting and harsh.

I'm amazed now that it never occurred to me that crying myself to sleep over something that had happened that day had become normal more nights than not. I was slowly becoming someone that I didn't recognize. I distinctly remember running into the bathroom at the church because I couldn't hold back the tears after a conversation in which someone attempted to encourage me, but all I heard was criticism.

The real Annette, the optimist to a fault, the happy-go-lucky life of the party, was transforming into an earnest, bitter, sadder person. There were still moments of the fun-loving, silly Annette—most often when I was in front of a group of kids "performing." But I was becoming a person I didn't like very much, and worst of all, I couldn't even see it.

Warning Sign 4: Isolation

Church work can be lonely. So many times I felt like I couldn't and shouldn't talk to anyone about my stress or my struggles. I so wanted to represent my church well, to not create division. I loved my church, and I didn't see anything to be gained by anyone knowing how much I struggled with people, policies, and workload.

There was something good and right about my desire to not stir up anxiety and negativity within the church. But I wasn't giving myself space to be human, a safe place to process my own sense of failure and confusion.

I thought I was doing my church a favor by keeping my struggles to myself, and in one sense I was. I was allowing others to continue to love the church without being burdened by news of what it's really like in the bowels of the church. So far so good.

But in the process of not sharing my inner struggles with church members, in the process of not burdening my family with what I was going through, I decided to not share my struggles with *anyone*. Isolation city. The longer I left my soul to fend for itself, the more likely I was to let my frustration seep out at just the wrong time.

Recovery and Beyond

I have talked to enough children's workers to know that some version of my experience is more common than we would like to admit. Too many children's ministers are hurt, confused, isolated, and lacking perspective, feeling "done," but seeing no way out.

At that time, the only way out I could see was to leave my position. Though I felt like a failure, like I was letting down people I dearly loved, I simply didn't have the prevention or recovery tools I needed to find my way out of the dark corner I had painted myself into.

But I'm so grateful that my ministry story doesn't end there. I'm so glad the end of the story is not me walking away from the church and from children's ministry altogether. (Though there were days when I seriously contemplated both!)

Now with the benefit of years of coaching children's ministry professionals, I have seen more than a few recover their sense of joy and calling, often without having to leave their ministries behind. So in honor of my courageous colleagues in children's ministry who have worked the recovery process much more honestly and faithfully than I did on my first shot at ministry, I offer these practices I have seen restore health to children's ministry workers just like us.

1. Isolation is not your friend. We all know—in our heads—that everyone needs a sounding board. When I was in emotional freefall, if you had asked me whether it was a good idea to isolate, I would have said an unequivocal no. If you had asked if I thought people needed to have coaches and counselors to stay healthy, I would have given you an absolute yes.

But when I felt like I was on the front lines, trying to put out a fire at a burning building, it never felt like the right time to take a break and talk about my feelings. But even ministry firefighters need a break and a place to express frustration, ask for encouragement, and even receive correction from someone they trust. But it's so hard to pull away from the work when everything seems so urgent and intense.

Another tricky part is actually finding the place to get support we need. When we're in a confused and discouraged place, we don't have the time or energy to ask for referrals, interview counselors and coaches, or even make an appointment with a trusted friend outside of the church.

Outside of your church and your immediate family, you'd be surprised by the wide variety of support available to you. Think of it this way: we want to build an ecosystem of wise, supportive friends, coaches, counselors, and spiritual directors who can give us perspective when we are losing ours. I'm going to suggest a few possibilities for you, but these ideas are not mutually exclusive. You likely need all of them, especially when you find yourself showing those important warning signs. Tragically, I availed myself of none of these means of support when I was crumbling around the edges.

* *A colleague in another church.* Some people find another children's minister nearby. Someone who understands your position can be a great source of encouragement and perspective for you.

* *Friends outside of ministry.* I have had friends who could hear my stories and feel my frustration with me, and because they are outside my ministry, they can give me a clearer perspective on what is really happening, and even let me know that I am overreacting at times.

* *A counselor.* A minister I know negotiated regular visits to a professional counselor into her salary package. Too many of us see visiting a counselor as evidence of failure rather than what it is—a way to protect our ministries from inflicting our unhealthy selves on them!

* *A coach.* Someone who has been in ministry a little longer than you has likely walked through some of the same struggles you have. I've heard Mark say that the healthiest people he knows in ministry have multiple coaches—a ministry coach, a marriage coach, a parenting coach, a life-planning coach, a financial coach, a physical health coach. Most of these will be volunteers, friends you prevail upon periodically to share their wisdom. But in some areas, we need a professional coach to help us move through a prickly situation or to the next level. (You can find information about finding a ministry coach by emailing info@ministryarchitects.com.)

2. Boundaries *is not a four-letter word.* Ministry—especially children's ministry—does not lend itself to a 9-to-5 lifestyle. Ministry happens when a child is sick and has been sent to the emergency room, when a volunteer cancels at 11 p.m. on a Saturday night, and when it's the night before VBS and there is still setup work to do.

Setting clear, reasonable, and flexible boundaries may be one of the biggest challenges the average children's minister faces. We know we've got to have boundaries around our time. Without boundaries, we end up sacrificing our family, our health, and our joy. But we also know there are times when our boundaries have to be interrupted. The trick is knowing when.

I like to start by putting a box around times when I won't be available for ministry: sabbath days, family nights, date nights with my husband. During these set times each week, I don't answer email of any kind (on my phone, computer, or iPad). Few people expect an immediate email response. A good rule of thumb is that an email response within twenty-four hours fits in the highly responsive category. If someone needs an immediate response, they can call or text you.

One of my biggest obstacles to setting boundaries is my phone. I can be on the couch enjoying a movie with my husband on a Saturday evening, and one little text could get me into work mode faster than I could say "I need to take care of this. It will just take a minute."

Too many nights I left him to finish a movie alone while I rushed off to fix something, which never takes just a minute. Each time felt like it was "just this once," but to him, I was *always* available to have our time interrupted by work. Not a good recipe for a healthy marriage or a healthy life.

Thankfully, he was generous enough to bring his hurt to my attention. I knew that I needed to change. We made the decision that there would be certain times when I turned off my phone. I can check it for emergencies just before I go to bed. I've discovered that there are very few ministry emergencies that can't wait a few hours for us to address them.

This practice saved a few friendships too. I would be out with friends, get a text or call about work, and leave my friends and tend to the call, which always took much longer than expected. While I felt so noble for sacrificing my time with my friends for ministry, they were annoyed, more convinced than ever that my life was out of control.

When it's my kids, when it's my husband, I answer. When it's a ministry call that comes during a time out, I let it go to voicemail.

The boundaries battle is won when we name the times each week when we will not be working. Although there will be times when we need to adjust, with a clear plan for off time, those times become the exception, not the rule. In chapter fourteen, I'll introduce you to a liberating practice we use with almost all our clients, called the Rhythmic Week.

3. *Take your medicine.* Proverbs 17:22 says, "A cheerful heart is good medicine." And modern research has proved it's actually true.

A study at Indiana State University found that laughter not only reduces stress but improves the survival rates for people with cancer. And University of Maryland researchers found a link between laughter and cardiovascular health. Laughter can give a miniworkout, getting our shoulders moving and contracting our abdominal muscles. It can help us breathe more deeply, stretching our lungs, reinvigorating our entire body.

When Jesus says that we must come like children (Mark 10:13-16), I wonder if he had laughter in mind. More seriousness and heaviness seldom brings the answer we're looking for. But when we bring buoyancy and joy, we are much more likely to come up with creative solutions to whatever has gotten us tied up in knots.

Watch or read something that makes you laugh, belly laugh. Make time for friends who have the same effect on you. As crazy as it sounds, this too can be a part of your intentional soul-tending regime. Have you taken your medicine today? I'm serious.

4. *There is life out there.* Every now and then kids will roll their eyes and say to one of their parents, "Mom [or Dad], get a life!" And when they do, we ought to listen.

When our lives become consumed with and defined by the obligations of family and ministry, we shrink. We become less interesting, less attractive, living in a shell and not experiencing the abundant life we claim to know.

For a long time I felt guilty for wanting to "get a life" outside of work and family. I would say, with just a smidge of pride, "I don't have time for anything else in my life." Really? No time for music or exercise or friends or hobbies or reading or movies or dance or . . . ?

When I decided to learn to play tennis, I discovered that I actually *was* able to make time, and that time actually expanded my world and my friendships. "Having a life" almost always makes us the kind of people who get more, not less, done. The mental break and the distance from the urgent and immediate has a way of energizing us for the work side of our lives.

5. *Come on in: the (living) water's fine.* We all got into children's ministry because we love Jesus and kids. But our schedules can suck the life out of our life in Christ. Instead of abiding, we find ourselves skimming. Instead of drinking deeply, we take a sip on the run.

Too many of us treat our busyness as our badge of honor. People say, "You sacrifice so much for your ministry, busy all the time taking care of all these children!" But Eugene Peterson challenges all of us in ministry: "The word *busy* is the symptom not of commitment but of betrayal. It is not devotion but defection. Busy set as a modifier to pastor should sound to our ears like adulterous to characterize a wife or embezzling to characterize a banker."

Let's get real here. Abiding in Christ doesn't come naturally to most of us. It is much easier to be pulled along by the rushing current of today's task list (which will, by the way, almost never get done).

Making intentional space for God begins when we fight for and begin to live into the "unforced rhythms of grace" (Matthew 11:29 *The Message*). I love the word *rhythm*. Everyone's rhythm will be a little different; we create our own intentional pattern that, at different times and in different ways, combines listening, Scripture, prayer, meditation, silence, singing, and journaling to amplify our confidence that this is first and foremost God's work.

Prevention and Recovery

Regardless of how long we've been in ministry, our daily choices can create chronic fatigue of the soul. If we are not choosing preventative disciplines to prevent burnout, emptiness, and injury, we will eventually need to make time—usually much *more* time—for a season of recovery.

I recently completed my second half marathon. The way I approached my second experience was vastly different from the first one. When I signed up for my first half marathon, I researched training plans, read articles on nutrition, and religiously followed the calendar of suggested runs. I was terrified that I wouldn't be ready on race day. Nevertheless, I had a great run, and it didn't take much to convince me to sign up for another.

But what happened to my body in the days following the race was anything but glorious. At first, my muscles were sore, which was to be expected. As the next few days passed, my back and my feet hurt to the point that I could hardly walk.

I didn't know what was happening. I made it through the race just fine. I was happy with my time. I thought the hard part was over.

I spent the next several weeks limping to and from chiropractic visits and back to the couch. I was in lots of pain, and pretty much worthless for a few weeks. I was still a little puzzled and confused.

I had followed the training plan explicitly, yet it seemed everything was falling apart. I went from running thirteen miles to barely getting across the living room.

I eventually learned I just *thought* I was following the training plan. The one piece I left out—I figured it was not really essential to the plan—was stretching. I hadn't stretched properly through my entire training plan. After most of my long runs, I was off to take care of the next thing on my list. Little did I know I was going to suffer so much. Just taking a few extra minutes after each run would have put me back in my running shoes so much sooner.

My second half marathon was different. I trained, but not as methodically as the first time. But I did invest in some preventative care, both equipment to help me stretch better and therapeutic massage to get the lactic acid out of my muscles. I wasn't willing to risk being down like that again. I ran that second half marathon with less hard training and more focus more on preventative measures.

What happened? I ran the second race faster than the first, and with almost no recovery time. I didn't miss a single day with my running shoes!

Ministry is not unlike running a marathon! We don't have to run on empty. Self-care is not selfish. In fact, it will likely have a more profound affect on your ministry than any ministry technique you will ever try.

Finding Your Bounce

*The Inside Secret of Sustainable
Children's Ministry*

> *I don't measure a man's success by how high he climbs
> but how high he bounces when he hits bottom.*
>
> GEORGE S. PATTON JR.

> *Balance. It's like a unicorn; we've heard about it,
> everyone talks about it and makes airbrushed T-shirts
> celebrating it, it seems super rad, but we haven't actually
> seen one. I'm beginning to think it isn't a thing.*
>
> JEN HATMAKER, FOR THE LOVE

Our church had always put on a large fall festival for the community. It was a full-blown *event* on an evening in October, complete with petting zoo, bands, carnival games, food, and fair rides.

Since we had always pulled off this event successfully for years, we decided to expand it from a couple hours into a full-day affair and to partner with other churches. What had once been an event in our church parking lot benefiting only our church would become a citywide outreach and benefit lots of churches. We were excited. The potential to impact and encourage our community was going to be exponentially more than our church working alone—or so we thought.

We scheduled an initial meeting with other churches in the area, and they were less than inspired by the idea. Our efforts to make this a multichurch sponsored event weren't going anywhere. The weight of our great idea for a massive community fair ended up resting solely on us. Our three partner churches did send a total of six volunteers (out of more than one hundred required for the event). But we were not discouraged. We forged ahead with our plans.

Finally, the day came. We were encouraged by a nice handful of people waiting when we opened up, but the food vendors were two hours late. Can you imagine a fall festival without food?

We had hired a great band. But we made the mistake of scheduling them to perform first. There might have been twenty-four people there to hear the band if we counted the volunteers who snuck away from their responsibilities to be in the audience. The vendors working one of the carnival games didn't speak a word of English and then ran out of the supplies they needed by just after noon. It seemed like nothing went as planned.

The turnout was much weaker than expected. In fact, we could have held it in our church's small parking lot. The crowd looked even smaller against the backdrop of a massive city park. And with low ticket sales, we had spent more money than we hoped to bring in. Our budget was totally blown.

We had dreamed big, really big. We had worked hard, but in the end we had embarrassed ourselves and our church partners in the process. This was a public flop in front of all the people who had volunteered, all the people who had contributed financially, all the people who had trusted us with this dream.

I hope you've never had to experience a failure this public or this epic. But if you stay in this work long enough, there's a good chance that you'll find yourself shaking your head at the disappointing end of a "great idea," wondering what in the world went wrong.

If we are doing our jobs, every now and then we'll be stretching ourselves, experimenting, innovating, and, yes, failing. Show me a children's minister who hasn't failed at something in the last few years, and I'll show you one who is trapped in "the way we've always done things."

The good news is that how we react to failure can be much more important than avoiding failure altogether. We can wallow in the wreckage of our best-laid plans, or we can learn to bounce. The good news is that resilience can be learned. The bad news is that the training exercises for developing grit and bounce almost always includes more opportunities for failure.

One of the benefits of having many ideas is that I get the chance to fail often and quickly. If there were such a degree, I sure I would have earned an involuntary PhD in resilience. (Please refer to me as Dr. Bounce for the rest of this book.) As one eminently qualified in the fine art of failure, let me offer a few steps out of the pit for those times you're not sure you can (or even want to) get up and try again.

1. Be humble. My instinctive first reaction to my own failure in ministry is to get defensive. When I've worked hard to put together an event or new initiative and something goes wrong, I want to blame someone. I understand, theoretically, that failure is a part of the process. But ooh, when it comes, it stings every time.

Maybe it was my fault; maybe someone else totally blew it. But when someone makes a critical comment, it's all I can do not to dive into rationalizing, justifying, and explaining (all ways of saying, "It wasn't my fault").

More often than not, though, the buck stops with me. Making excuses never helps and usually multiplies the criticism. Defensiveness has a way of fueling criticism even more. As hard as it is, I try to welcome criticism, take a few notes for next time, and respond with "Fair enough" or "Point well taken."

2. *If you pay the tuition, learn the lesson.* Every failure costs something. It may cost our pride, our confidence, or the trust of those around us. I like to see every failure as tuition paid for my education in leadership and ministry. So if we pay the tuition, let's learn everything there is to learn from the course! There's a lesson in every flop.

At the end of every failed operation, I typically want to pretend that it never happened. The last thing I want to do is debrief. But debriefing is exactly the step you'll need to take if you don't want to repeat the same mistakes again.

When we pull together a listening group to gather feedback "for next time," it will likely be painful to be reminded of the places where we missed the mark. But debriefs can also get folks thinking ahead with solutions for improvement, rather than just looking back at our mistakes.

3. *Talk most about what you want most.* Here's a profound principle for life and ministry: we always get more of what we focus on. If our focus is on mentally chewing our mistakes over and over again, we'll likely get more mistakes. If we focus on what we want to see come next or the ways that God works in spite of our foibles, we'll be more attentive to God at work.

Once we have a handle on what went wrong and how to improve next time (if there is a next time), we can continue to celebrate the things that *are* going well. I'm not talking about pretending everything is great, but owning up to our failures and not allowing our entire life and ministry be defined by a couple of misses. We can set the atmosphere by choosing to focus first on the ways God *is* at work regardless of our most recent misstep.

Fail fast. Fail forward. Once you've had the chance to practice the resilience strategy a few dozen times, the sting of failure may not go away but it won't be quite as sharp. And one day you may become a failure ninja like me!

Your Constellation of Coaches

One of the keys to longevity and joy in ministry is the constellation of coaches and mentors you build into your life and ministry. As you're building your own bounce strategy, take a minute right now to assess your mentors and coaches, along with anyone you are currently mentoring.

If you're not satisfied with your list, write the names of five people you could ask out for coffee or a meal over the next month to see if they might serve as formal or informal mentors or coaches for you in the coming year. Here I want to introduce you to the various types of people who might provide the healthy support, training, and coaching you will need.

1. Ministry mentors. Sure, we can learn from our own mistakes. Personally, I prefer to learn from someone else's! Someone else has already paid the tuition, and I'd love to learn from them.

Most of the children's ministry leaders I know haven't had much in the way of formal ministry training. Few have studied children's ministry in college or seminary. Most haven't gone to a single children's ministry workshop. The best leaders, are, of course, learners. But too often we're so caught up in chasing the details of our ministry that we see training for ourselves a luxury we can't afford.

Let me put it as clearly as I can. If you hope to stay energized, alive, and effective in ministry for the long haul, ongoing learning is not an option you can afford to be without. Experience doesn't necessarily train us, especially when our experience serves to calcify us in doing the exact same things in the exact same way.

Whether you've been in ministry two months or twenty years, I recommend that you build two strategic relationships into your life:

you should always be mentoring someone, and you should always have a mentor. When you provide mentoring, you can't help but become wiser and clearer in your ministry skills. And if you take the counsel of a person mentoring you, you *will* grow, even if their advice isn't always perfectly on target.

Mrs. Geni began to teach me about children's ministry when I taught my first Sunday school lesson at eleven years old. She taught me piano when I was a teen, but between the scales we spent a good chunk of that time talking about life. She had a profound influence on my faith, my love of music, and my ministry.

When I returned to Dallas for grad school, I worked for Mrs. Geni part-time, coordinating the midweek children's ministry at our church. We met at least once a month, and she would share what she knew about leadership and organization, teaching me about ministry systems the whole time.

When I took the leadership of a children's ministry in the same town decades later, guess where I went for help? Mrs. Geni even sponsored a children's ministry training conference, involving children's ministry leaders from churches from all around the area. I brought my best and brightest leaders to her meetings so they too could learn the systems she practiced that allowed her to keep so many plates spinning at one time.

At times, I have invited different people to formally mentor me. But I quickly realized that I didn't have to formally define someone as a mentor to pick up incredible wisdom from them. I often reached out to friends whose lives and ministries I deeply respected.

2. Supervisors. As you embark on a position in a new church, your supervisor will play a huge role in your development. Especially early on, it's great to have a supervisor willing to spend time with you every week to help you learn about the culture of the church and to hold you accountable to the priorities that matter most to them.

Your supervisor can warn of you landmines, give you invaluable pastoral care information about families in your ministry, and help you get the right things done without ruffling the wrong feathers. This person doesn't need to know a lot about children's ministry. You have been hired as the resident expert in that field. But your supervisor is the expert on the expectations the congregation and staff have for your position.

At the same time, having a supervisor as a mentor can be complicated and tricky. Assuming they will be a mentor to you is usually a recipe for disappointment. Your supervisor's biggest job is to *supervise* you, to make sure you are doing your job, not to disciple, coach, or provide spiritual direction for you. Get the first part of the relationship clear (the supervising part), and the other three might just come in its wake.

3. Coaches. The coaches you build into your life can have a huge impact on your ability to bounce back from the certain setbacks of ministry. Executive coaching has become a multibillion dollar industry in the world of business. There's a reason why almost all Olympians have a coach in their corner. Coaching makes us better.

A great coach will bring just the right combination of encouragement and pressure, putting the right tension on the string so your life and ministry is in tune. There is only one kind of children's minister who doesn't need a coach—one who doesn't want to grow or get better. It will be a total waste of that person's time.

The distinction we tend to make between mentors and coaches is that mentors primarily *respond* to your invitations to meet. A coach takes more initiative to help you identify your goals and help you achieve them. A coach also typically focuses on a single area of your life—finances, ministry, or health—while a mentor might be more focused on you as a person. Though not always, coaching tends to be a formalized relationship and mentoring is more informal.

Developing a Community of Support

When you are in the unique position of being on a church staff, community can be hard to come by. There are times when it will be wildly inappropriate and unhelpful for you to share your frustrations about ministry or the tension you feel with members of your team or colleagues on your church's staff. But you will not likely last long through the messy chapters of ministry without a community of support. So where will you find it?

Unfortunately, most of us are anything but intentional about the communities we build around ourselves. It is possible, though, to create for ourselves a life-giving constellation of friends who together provide for us a healthy ecosystem we can do ministry within.

I'm coming to realize that friends outside of my own ministry, outside of my own church, can have a profound effect on me and my ministry. In addition to more formal coaches and mentors, I want to make sure I've always got the following kinds of people in my life:

* friends in ministry in my own community who are in churches like mine

* friends working in ministries different from my own

* friends who lead mission and nonprofit work I am passionate about in my community

* safe friends, certainly outside my church, often outside my town, who I can vent to and unload in ways I can't and shouldn't with those inside my own faith community

* wise friends and family members

* leaders within my church who serve in other areas of ministry— deacons, elders, small group leaders, church staff members

Don't worry. These are not necessarily relationships you'll be tending to every week or even every month. One of the most life-giving communities of support I have is the team of fellow consultants at Ministry Architects. Once a year I get to meet with fifteen to twenty of them on an annual retreat. We might not touch base throughout the entire year, but this group of friends profoundly shapes the way I now do life and ministry.

When we surround ourselves primarily with those in the children's ministry worlds, our ministries suffer for it. We may think we are focusing by not having a community outside of our children's ministry team, but we're actually ensuring that our next year's ministry will be a shrinking version of the one we're leading today.

For the Long Haul

To some people, the children's ministry journey has felt like a royal game of bait and switch. For many of us, leading a children's ministry at first sounded like a fun way to share with kids what a life with Jesus might be like.

It didn't take long, though, before I realized how little time I was spending *with* children, maybe only 10 percent of ministry time. The other 90 percent was managing the people, systems, and projects that make ministry happen.

Remember the architect, general contractor, and laborer roles I defined in chapter eight? For the vast majority of our time, we serve as general contractors, making sure everyone has the tools they need to do their jobs. If you began as most of us did, as a "laborer" in the class with kids every Sunday and preparing a weekly craft, and if you now lead a ministry that requires multiple volunteers each week, you've probably had to let go of quite a few of the laborer tasks that got you into this work to begin with.

This shift may be the *single biggest struggle* for the children's ministers I get to coach. Their ministry success depends largely on whether they can make the leap from being a leader to being a leader of leaders. Leaders who can't seem to make the switch from laborer to general contractor are destined to struggle year after year trying to keep their heads above water until they burn out, quit, or get fired.

When I met Gina, she was in her sixteenth year of children's ministry, having been children's ministry director in several churches. She knew the world of children's ministry well, but after a year at her new church, things were still "falling apart." She was working seventy hours a week or so and was running herself ragged just to get through the week. She stepped into her position on the heels of a well-loved children's ministry director, and the church was not adjusting well to the change. She had not been welcomed with open arms.

She struggled to get volunteers and felt like she was a victim of a negative church culture. She lacked the systems she needed to shift out of her laborer role. She couldn't imagine doing ministry differently.

When we first met, she had serious doubts about the process. I'll give her credit; she opened herself to the process, but she was still skeptical that anything could really change. She had a big job ahead of her. Not only did she need to overcome the church's own lack of enthusiasm and investment in the children's ministry, she would need to be willing to hand off some of the laborer tasks she had mastered so well. She would need to live with the discomfort of knowing that, at least for a while, the tasks she handed off would not be done as well she had been doing them.

But she knew that if she was going to stay in her position, she would need to cut her workload almost in half. She struggled as she worked the recruiting process, returning naturally to the negative narratives that had been burned into her brain.

* People won't volunteer no matter how many times I ask.

* Parents care more about soccer than church.

* I leave messages, but nobody responds to my emails and voicemails.

* People won't commit months before we need them.

But week after week, she worked the recruiting process outlined in chapter nine. It wasn't so much that it was time consuming (in fact, this process wound up taking far less time than she had spent in previous years) as much as it was totally different and therefore often uncomfortable. She started building her volunteer team a full six months before she needed them. In her mind, starting the recruiting process this early was totally unnecessary and a complete waste of her time. But it worked. She had all the volunteers she needed by her Sunday school kickoff in the fall.

But recruiting her team was only half the battle. Now that she had a team, she had to equip them to play their positions well. Over the next several months she had built a children's ministry leadership team that met with her once a month.

Their transition to taking on load-bearing responsibility did not happen immediately. Meeting once a month, it took several months for the team to move beyond just giving Gina advice and into carrying real leadership. Without knowing it, Gina had trained them to expect their children's ministry staff person to do the vast majority of the work, rather than to equip the congregation to do the work.

But Gina presented the same model of ministry to them every meeting until it began to stick. By consistently, steadily, persistently clarifying each team member's role, most of them began to catch the vision that the children's ministry belonged to the church, not just to its staff.

I did say "most" of them. Some resisted the change and chose to end their volunteer commitment early. I had to keep reminding Gina that she was right on track. When healthy leaders lead well, not everyone will get on board. In fact, some will strenuously resist. In this case, we assured her, the resistance was a sign she was doing something *right*!

As Gina built a new team who embraced a new vision for a shared children's ministry, she started to find freedom in her schedule. Within six months, and with a little strategic coaching through the slick spots, Gina had delegated enough of her laborer roles that she was now working twenty fewer hours a week—still more than full-time, but a huge improvement!

She was inching her way back into a sustainable pace of life work. And more importantly, she was architecting a shift in the culture surrounding the children's ministry, learning to pay attention and tell better stories about the work God was doing in children, parents, and volunteers. Her excitement about what the team was accomplishing was contagious.

If you walk into her church now, you will find a woman who has grown as a leader, and you will find families excited to participate in ministry together. It took Gina almost two years to make the shift out of her laborer role and into the general contractor role. But as we told her, "Shifting a culture in two years is about one year ahead of schedule!"

In appendix G, you will find a template that over time will help you incorporate all of the systems in this book. We call it the "Children's Ministry Systems Checklist."

On Juggling: A Final Word

As we had to remind Gina many times, the process works when we are willing to work the process. It's no surprise that the juggler has become an image so many of us use for the work we're in. We're trying to keep all the balls in the air at the same time, trying not to drop any of them, though more balls keep getting thrown at us all the time.

I remember seeing Jeff Dunn-Rankin, from our Ministry Architects team, offer a radical alternative to the anxious juggling that I and most of my children's ministry friends had grown so comfortable doing. Jeff asks if anyone in the audience knows how to juggle. Every now and then a brave volunteer admits they juggle "a little." Jeff brings the volunteer forward for a demonstration and asks, "Can you juggle one more ball?" Almost always the juggler says no. But Jeff immediately responds with "Just try," and he throws another ball to the juggler.

Something always gets dropped—usually it's everything. Jeff quickly picks up all the balls and says enthusiastically, "Let's try again!" He repeats the process several more times, tossing additional balls at the juggler, until all the balls are on the floor. Again. (Maybe this is why Jeff doesn't have many friends.)

Then Jeff says, "I'm actually a pretty good juggler myself," and he brings out a basket of a couple dozen balls and shows them to the group. "How many of these do you think I can juggle at one time?" he asks.

Before the group can agree on an answer, he says, "I can keep them all in the air at the same time. Would you like to see?"

The curious audience responds positively. Jeff, to the immediate groaning response of the crowd, places each ball in the hand of a different audience member, asking everyone to keep tossing their balls in the air. Jeff keeps one for himself and tosses it in the air, proudly announcing, "And *this* is how I juggle two dozen balls at the same time!"

My dear friend in ministry, if you have made it this far, I know you and I are kindred spirits. We know this work that we have been given is too important for us to spend our hours scrambling and flailing, trying to keep up with the dozens of balls being thrown at us each day.

The beautiful news is that we can do more than react. We don't have to be driven by the screaming urgencies of ministry. We can live at a life-giving pace and lead inspired teams who are deeply passionate about the ministry Jesus warned us not to ignore. We can build systems and use tools that will allow us to do exponentially more than we could ever do without them.

Just ask Gina.

Acknowledgments

From Annette:

Geni Brooks—for taking a chance on an awkward eleven-year-old who loved Jesus and wanted to learn to teach kids how great he is. Your ministry reaches far beyond the walls of your own church.

My parents, John and Cheryl Grey—for teaching me to love church and the God who loves us, and for being my unabashed cheerleaders.

My husband, Kevin—for supporting me and believing in me through the difficult times and making space for me grow into the woman you knew I could become. For seeing a bright future that I couldn't. And for making sure the kids got some real food while I finished this project.

Shari Boyd—for walking through the fire with me and trusting me enough to try again after our burns had healed. I love and admire you more than you know. You are a rock star.

Mark DeVries—for moving outside of the youth ministry world by saying yes to churches who asked for a systems approach for their children's ministries. Thank you for allowing me to partner in this project.

Jeff Dunn-Rankin—for your ear, your prayers, and sharing your unique and wise perspective over and over again.

Debbie Freeman—for your feedback and support from the infancy of this project, and for your grace-filled honesty and friendship.

From Mark:

I am acutely grateful for my pastors, George and Trish Holland, who were relentlessly with me and for me as I grew up under the shelter of their incomparable kindness.

Adam, Debbie, and Leigh, you let me practice children's ministry on you and keep giving me grace as I stumble into the delights of being your dad.

I can only pray that my four grandchildren, Parish, Nealy, Liam, and Jack, will be shaped and formed in Christ by communities of faith wise enough to disproportionately invest in the next generation.

To the saints at First Presbyterian Church, Nashville, Tennessee— I do not have enough years left to say thank you enough for what you have done for my children.

Annette, thanks for diving into this project with your heart wide open, even if you're eyes weren't. You never gave up and kept nudging us forward every time we got stuck. It's that quality that makes you a one-of-a-kind consultant.

Appendix A

Communication Plan

Objective

To establish normative processes for effective and timely communication with parents, children, and leaders utilizing targeted communication strategies that can be regularly updated as more is learned about the most effective communication mechanisms for each audience.

This plan establishes a baseline, a consistent rhythm of communication that can and should be supplemented as the needs of specific events and new initiatives arise. It is understood that the children's ministry will draw on a wide variety of communication methods, including the church website, Facebook, texting, print marketing, snail mail, email, Instagram, and so on.

Foundational Content

* At least twice a year (January and July), the children's ministry staff does a thorough review and update of the content and structure of the children's ministry webpages, ensuring that the following information is up-to-date and accurate:

    o Major children's ministry event calendar

    o Weekly programming times and locations

    o FAQs for new families ("What You Can Expect")

        ▪ the check-in process

- screening for volunteers
- how to get involved
- programming for parents
- pick up, snow day, and other policies

○ Pictures, brief bio(s), and contact information for children's ministry staff

○ Readily accessible "Contact Us" option

○ Pictures, video, or testimony of children, parents, and volunteers

* In time for the launch of the fall program (by July), the content from the website is summarized in a printed brochure, designed specifically to introduce new families to the children's ministry and to answer their questions. This piece should direct new families to the website for more detailed information and include at least the following information:

○ Who to call for more information

○ What to expect on your first visit

○ Major event calendar

○ Weekly programming calendar

* One often-neglected piece is ensuring that the children's ministry database is up-to-date and nimble, giving the children's ministry staff and key volunteers easy access to all the contact information they will need to communicate effectively with children, youth, and parents.

Regular Parent Communication

* Weekly social media updates (Facebook, Twitter, Instagram, or other platforms—not all of them) posted by a volunteer every Thursday o lesson topics

o special recognitions and celebrations

* Weekly website updates by a volunteer each Monday

* Director sends monthly email to parents with information about upcoming events, lessons, and a link to accompanying ebook or article for families

Communication with Children

* All children receive a postcard on their birthday from their Sunday school teacher, and can receive a special gift if they bring the postcard back to church. A volunteer makes sure the appropriate, addressed birthday cards are given to the appropriate teachers each week.

* All children receive a card from their Sunday school teacher within the first six weeks of the beginning of school. A volunteer makes sure that the appropriate, addressed cards are given to the appropriate teachers each week.

* The director reviews attendance at the beginning of each month, and children who have been missing for four weeks or more receive a call from their Sunday school teacher.

Communication with Volunteers

* The director or age-level coordinator sends a text or places a phone call each Thursday to each volunteer scheduled to serve that weekend, asking what the team can pray for and offering to answer questions.

* The director or age-level coordinator sends teachers an electronic copy of lesson plans the last week of the month for the following month.

* The director or age-level coordinator sends a weekly email every Thursday with info on curriculum, events, and a helpful teaching tip.

* Volunteer events are marketed by personal invitation, beginning at least six weeks prior to the event.

* The director or age-level coordinator sends each volunteer a card on his/her birthday.

Visual Communication

* Bulletin boards or wall space with posters show weekly/monthly lesson topics, children's birthdays or special recognition, and seasonal inspiration.

* Hallway screens display a loop of slides announcing upcoming events, lesson topics, and volunteers to be celebrated.

Foundational Event Promotion

* *Website.* The event is announced on the website at least three months prior to the actual event, with new promotional content being added to the website every two weeks, until two weeks after the event.

* *Newsletter.* The event is highlighted in the church newsletter one month prior to the event itself, drawing on the content created over the previous three months on the website.

* *Postcards or fliers.* Two weeks prior to the event, any print promotion is put in the mail.

* *Personal calls and emails.* Two weeks prior to the event, personal calls and emails are assigned to key staff and volunteers. These personal contacts continue until the event has received the targeted number of RSVPs.

* *Email.* One week prior to the event, two group emails are sent:
    o reminding those who have RSVP'd
    o giving a final invitation to those who have not yet signed up
* *Email recap and thank you.* This email goes out to all participants and volunteers within one week after the event, with information about a selected upcoming program.

Sample Goals and Benchmarks

Target Goal Anniversary Date: December 31, 2020
Target Benchmark Anniversary Date: December, 31, 2018

Sample Goal 1

2020 Goal: An enhanced ministry will be in place to welcome and support children with special needs for all services and programs of the church.

2018 Benchmark: A game plan has been adopted to support and welcome children with special needs.

Sample Goal 2

2020 Goal: The children's ministry will serve an average of fifty children a week in one of its weekly programs over the previous year.

2018 Benchmark: The children's ministry has served an average of twenty children a week in one of its weekly programs over the previous year.

Sample Goal 3

2020 Goal: All programs and classrooms are supported with appropriate technology and infrastructure.

2018 Benchmark: A classroom-needs list has been presented to the appropriate decision-making bodies, and a plan is in place to meet these needs.

Sample Goal 4

2020 Goal: Over the previous year, the children's ministry will provide quarterly opportunities for parents to learn how to become the primary faith developer for their children.

2018 Benchmark: One parent-equipping event has taken place in the previous year, and at least two more events have been calendared for the upcoming year.

Sample Goal 5

2020 Goal: Over the previous year, five new off-site service opportunities will be offered for children to give them the opportunity to give back to the community.

2018 Benchmark: Over the previous year, elementary children have been given the opportunity to serve outside the walls of the church in service projects, and over twenty children have participated.

Appendix C

Sample Values Statements

Most churches choose three or four core values. The following are some samples from several different churches.

Sample 1

* *Christ-centered.* Everything we do comes from an intentional desire to follow Christ and his teachings as found in the Bible.

* *Accepting.* We seek to embrace, welcome, and minister to all children and their families just as Christ modeled for us.

* *Welcoming.* We cultivate an atmosphere of Christian hospitality for all.

* *Equipping.* We equip children with the knowledge and ability to continue their lifelong, intentional practice of faith.

* *Love.* We welcome everyone with the love of Jesus Christ.

* *Spiritual growth.* We nurture a foundation of faith in children and families, focusing on personal growth and a relationship with Christ.

* *Discipleship.* We provide opportunities for children to encounter Jesus Christ through Scripture-based experiences in worship, learning, and service for the purpose of preparing faithful disciples of Christ.

* *Engaging.* We encourage children to internalize God's Word through innovative age-appropriate experiences and programming.

* *Nurturing.* We reflect God's love and encourage children, through loving and compassionate interaction, to develop a personal relationship with Jesus Christ.

* *Relevant.* We will focus our curriculum and programs to be centered on the teachings of God's Word and how they apply to today's culture.

* *Serving others.* We will provide opportunities for children and youth to serve others in their daily life as a part of their faith journey.

* *Mission minded.* We will instill a willingness and desire to share the gospel in "Jerusalem, in Judea, and to the ends of the earth."

* *Dedication.* We demonstrate through our prayers, presence, gifts, and service our commitment to raise our children to be people of spiritual fervor.

Sample 2

* *Love* God and love others.
* *Grow* in faith together.
* *Serve* our community and our world.

Appendix D

Core Competencies Samples

Sample 1

The children of (name of church) will have gained knowledge and experience in the following areas:

A. Biblical Knowledge/Literacy

1. key stories

2. story of Christ

3. structure of the Bible

4. how to study the Bible

B. Christian Living

1. an example of Christ

2. confident in faith identity

3. how to pray

4. relying on your church family

C. Serving Others/Outreach

1. respect the dignity of all human beings

2. compassion

3. faith in action

D. Denominational Traditions

1. origins of the church

2. sacraments

3. elements of a service

4. connection to others through liturgy

5. saints and their stories

Sample 2

The children's ministry of (name of church) strives to develop children who

Know

* basic Bible stories

* the meaning of the sacraments

* children's hymns and Bible songs

* their pastors

Feel

* comforted in times of hardship

* confident in their faith, giftings, and who they are in Christ

* loved

Do

* ask questions about Bible interpretation

* actively participate in the life of the church

* live by the Golden Rule

* serve others

* participate in family rituals and Christian practices

Sample 3

The children of (name of church) will

Know

* the character of God

* God's plan of salvation, both for individuals and the world

* the blessing of life in Christ

Feel

* connected to Jesus, knowing their identity in Christ

* loved by God and the people of (name of church)

* compassion toward others

Do

* read, study, and memorize the Bible

* develop and abide in a personal relationship with Jesus Christ

* live the mission of (name of church)

  o love God

  o love others

  o go and make disciples

* encourage one another

Appendix E

Resources for Parents

Family Faith Talk Resources

* *One Year of Dinner Table Devotions and Discussion Starters* by Nancy Guthrie

* *Faith Conversations for Families* by Jim Burns

* *Instant Family Devotions* by Mike Nappa and Jill Wuellner

* *The Jesus Storybook Bible* by Sally Lloyd-Jones

* *Once-a-Day at the Table Family Devotional* by Christopher Hudson

* *Family Talk: Faith Edition* by Continuum Games

* *Kids Pack—Visual Faith Printed Card Set* by Vibrant Faith

Parenting Class Resources

* *Making Children Mind Without Losing Yours* by Kevin Leman

* Positive Parenting Solutions, www.positiveparentingsolutions .com

* Love and Logic, www.loveandlogic.com

* *Pass It On: Building a Legacy of Faith for Your Children Through Practical and Memorable Experiences* by Jim Burns

Preventative Maintenance Calendar

January Major Events

* The children's ministry major event calendar for the year has been updated.

* The children's ministry website has been reviewed and updated.

* The following forms have been updated:

  o volunteer covenants

  o medical forms

  o medication release form

  o liability forms

* Met with the coordinators for the summer events to go over details of their events and orient them to the notebooks for those events.

* All the details for March's events have been finalized.

February Major Events

* Volunteer recruiting season has opened.

  o Volunteer job descriptions have been reviewed and updated as necessary.

o All volunteer needs have been identified in the children's ministry through May, 15 months away.

o A recruiting-pool list has been developed with at least three times as many names as there are volunteer needs for the coming year.

o The recruiting pool has been ranked (ABC, and "with kids," "behind the scenes," or "either one") has been completed.

o Current volunteers have been contacted to determine whether they would like to serve again in the coming year.

o At least one potential leader's name has been placed by every open position on the volunteer needs list.

* Plans have begun for April events, and promotion has begun.

* Leadership training meetings for volunteers for the coming year have been calendared.

* The Children's Ministry Manual has been reviewed and updated as necessary.

March Major Events

* The committee/team for Promotion Sunday has been recruited.

* Recruiting of all partner volunteers for the coming year is 50 percent completed.

* Planning for the May events has started and promotion has begun.

* Met with the coordinator for VBS to go over details of the event and give out the notebook for that event.

* Updated curriculum has been ordered and plans are in place to distribute lessons to teachers at minimum of two weeks in advance of when lessons are needed.

* Plans and lessons for summer Sunday school have been selected and ordered.

* Plans have begun for May events, and promotion has begun.

* A news article has been written about a successful children's event for the church newsletter.

April Major Events

* Plans have begun for Promotion Sunday as well as the fall launch volunteer training meetings.

* Recruiting of all partner volunteers for the coming year is 75 percent completed.

* All special event coordinators have been recruited through the next eighteen months.

* Plans and lessons for summer Sunday school have been scheduled.

* Plans have begun for the June events, and promotion has begun.

* All curriculum resources for the coming year have been selected.

   o research and choosing of resources

   o creation of a schedule for Sunday school

* A check-in meeting with the summer-events coordinators has taken place to see how plans are coming along and to wrap up any dangling assignments.

May Major Events

* Summer event details have been finalized.

* Recruiting of all partner volunteers for the coming year is 90 percent completed.

* A volunteer thank you event has taken place.

* A promotional article about the summer's events has been written for the church's newsletter.

* Plans have begun for the July events, and promotion has begun.

June Major Events

* Processes have been established for collecting updated contact information for children and their families.

* Recruiting of all partner volunteers in the children's ministry has been completed.

* Curriculum resources for the coming year have been ordered.

* Plans have begun for the August events, and promotion has begun.

* The VBS coordinator and the VBS team have received all the support they need to run an effective event.

July Major Events

* Calls and emails have been sent to begin the children's ministry database updating process.

* Participation goals for the next year have been set, and processes have been put in place to achieve them.

* The children's ministry website has been reviewed and updated.

* The Promotion Sunday packet is complete with all forms, calendars, notices, etc.

* Plans have been finalized for the September events, and promotion has begun.

* All details for Promotion Sunday have been wrapped up.

August Major Events

* Promotion Sunday has taken place and Sunday school has begun.

* A volunteer training has taken place (orientation, CPR/first aid).

* The data for children and their families for the upcoming year's children's ministry directory has been updated, and directories have been distributed.

* The Children's Ministry Manual has been reviewed, and all documents have been updated.
* Plans have begun for the Christmas events.
* Plans have begun for the October events, and promotion has begun.
* Parent Interest Survey has been updated and distributed to parents.

September Major Events

* The year's expenses have been tallied, noting where spending was over or under budget. That information has been kept for next year's budget process.
* An article has been written about a successful children's event this fall for the church newsletter.
* Plans have begun for the November events, and promotion has begun.
* Parent Interest Surveys have been collected and parents have been plugged into the program.

October Major Events

* The children's ministry budget has been completed and turned in to the appropriate person(s).
* Details have been finalized for the children's ministry Christmas events.
* Plans have begun for the December events, and promotion has begun.
* Promotion for the Christmas event has begun.
* A Christmas event team has been recruited and oriented to their work together.

November Major Events

* The children's ministry MIA list has been reviewed with staff and follow-up calls have been made to all families who have been not been engaged in the previous year.

* A contact plan for the children's ministry has been updated, ensuring a regular rhythm of contact with parents, children, and volunteers.

* Met with the spring event coordinators to begin planning.

* Plans have begun for the January events, and promotion has begun.

December Major Events

* All major event notebooks for the events in the next year have been updated by the coordinators and collected by the staff.

* This month's children's ministry expenses have been tallied by creating a list of all expenses, which event or program they were for, what was actually purchased and paid for, and how much was spent.

* Plans for next summer have begun, and major summer events have been calendared.

* Plans have begun for the February events, and promotion has begun.

* A news article has been written about a successful children's event for the church newsletter.

Appendix G

Systems Checklist

Stage 1: Simple Machines

ACTION ITEM	TARGET DATE	POINT PERSON
☐ Update children's ministry directory and database	_____	_____
☐ Create a twelve-month major event calendar	_____	_____
☐ Develop a volunteer needs list (partners, including weekly leaders and major event coordinators)	_____	_____
☐ Create a recruiting pool list	_____	_____
☐ Names: behind the scenes, with kids, or both	_____	_____
☐ Rating: A, B, C	_____	_____
☐ Draft/update volunteer and staff job descriptions	_____	_____
☐ Children's ministry communication plan:	_____	_____

    1. Identifying communications coordinator

    2. Website

    3. Social media

    4. Bulletin board

    5. Church publications

☐ Select a "good enough"
curriculum and schedule its
lessons through the rest of the year   _____   _____

☐ Evaluate and update safety
and security policy   _____   _____

☐ Develop a visitor welcome
and follow-up process   _____   _____

☐ Develop a facilities and
equipment maintenance plan   _____   _____

☐ Develop a volunteer training
and equipping plan   _____   _____

Stage 2: Power Tools

ACTION ITEM   **TARGET DATE**   **POINT PERSON**

☐ Recruit a Volunteer
Leadership Team   _____   _____

☐ Recruit major event coordinators   _____   _____

☐ Develop visioning documents   _____   _____

    1. mission statement

    2. values

    3. year revolving goals with one-year benchmarks

    4. organizational chart: including who will play the roles of the
architect, general contractor, and skilled laborer(s)

☐ Gain buy-in/approval for the
visioning documents from key
stakeholders, including the senior
pastor, elders, etc.   _____   _____

☐ Develop a list of core
competencies (birth-fifth grade) _____ _____

☐ Contact every child in the children's
ministry (personal note) _____ _____

☐ Learn the names of every child
in the children's ministry _____ _____

☐ Contact every parent of a child
in the children's ministry _____ _____

Stage 3: Begin to Build

ACTION ITEM   **TARGET DATE**   **POINT PERSON**

☐ Schedule regular volunteer
leader gatherings _____ _____

☐ Begin one-on-one or one-on-two
face-to-face volunteer meetings _____ _____

☐ Develop a long-term staffing plan
(to provide capacity to achieve
the three-year goals) _____ _____

☐ Develop a master recruiting
needs list (helpers) _____ _____

☐ Develop a master curriculum
plan that addresses each of
the core competencies _____ _____

☐ Compile a Children's
Ministry Manual _____ _____

☐ Develop and update
compliance documents: _____ _____
(music and video copyright licensing, background checks, child
protection policies, etc.)

☐ Create major event notebooks _____ _____

☐ Create a preventative
  maintenance calendar   _____ _____

Stage 4: Finishing Touches

ACTION ITEM	TARGET DATE	POINT PERSON
☐ Schedule parent engagement events	_____	_____
☐ Develop a plan for integrating children into the life of the larger church	_____	_____
☐ Execute one high impact/high visibility program	_____	_____
☐ Update children's ministry facilities	_____	_____

Appendix H

For Reflection and Discussion

Introduction

1. From just reading the introduction, what topics do you think are most important for your children's ministry right now?

2. What questions are you bringing to the reading of this book?

3. After reading the Introduction, do you have any concerns that this might not be the book you thought it would be? If so, what are those concerns?

Chapter 1: From Chaos to Clarity

1. How would you describe the current health of your children's ministry?

2. If you could build a ministry from scratch, what would you do differently from what you are doing now?

3. Which of the symptoms of system deficiency are most prevalent in your ministry?

4. Think about your volunteers. How do they express their concern about the symptoms you identified in question 3?

Chapter 2: The Workhorse Syndrome

1. Have you ever felt a twinge of resentment about the workload you carry in the children's ministry?

2. Review the symptoms of the Workhorse Syndrome. Which of those resonate most with you?

3. If you were to focus on doing the things that only you can do, what three things would you stop doing?

4. What have you sacrificed to finish a project or meet a deadline that you wish you hadn't sacrificed?

Chapter 3: Beyond Goldfish and Bubble Machines

1. Are there things you have done in your ministry that felt like they were just "icing," sweet and pretty, but lacking substance?

2. How did you feel reading about the dance floor? Which parts of the story, if any, particularly resonated with you?

3. What systems did you hear in Catie's story that you are already using? Which ones would be most helpful to put in place?

4. What from your ministry do you hope will remain after you have moved out of your leadership role?

Chapter 4: Measuring Up

1. How did you feel reading about setting a target number for growth in your ministry?

2. What would it look like to grow by 10 percent? By 50 percent? How would you staff for that size ministry? What would have to change about what you are doing now to support that kind of growth?

3. How does your ministry compare to the norms listed in this chapter:

   o Budget?

   o Staff?

   o Volunteers?

   o Percent of worshiping congregation?

4. What can you do to champion the importance of the children's ministry to the rest of your church?

Chapter 5: Building Your Ministry with Simple Machines

1. Have you experienced any of the symptoms of a stuck ministry listed at the beginning of the chapter? Were you able to get unstuck? If so, how?

2. Which of the simple machines do you already have in place?

3. What is keeping you from implementing the systems you are lacking?

4. Which system, if you had it up and running, would eliminate the most stress from your ministry?

Chapter 6: From Pearls to a Necklace

1. What are some of the pearls in your children's ministry?

2. What is the process for updating and adding information to your church's website?

3. Which pieces of essential information listed in this chapter are already on your website, and which ones have yet to be added?

4. How many formats for communication are you currently using? Can you think of a few new ones to add?

5. What is the current state of your database, and what will it take to update the information on children and families?

6. How often do volunteers receive training on your safety policies?

Chapter 7: Seeing What Others Can't—Yet

1. Does your children's ministry have a mission statement? If so, how do you communicate it to parents, volunteers, and church members?

2. How would you describe the spirit of your ministry? How do you think your parents and volunteers would describe it?

3. How would your ministry change if your programming revolved around a set of specific competencies? Would your events change at all? What about your weekly programming? Why?

4. What milestone events does your church currently celebrate for children? Are there some you would like to add?

Chapter 8: The Delegation Dance

1. As you read the descriptions of the architect, general contractor, and skilled laborers, which role do you most identify with and why?

2. Think about some of the tasks that don't give you joy. Which of those could you ask a volunteer to take off of your plate?

3. If you already have a children's ministry team, what ideas do you have from this chapter about how to more effectively utilize them?

4. If you don't have a children's ministry team, which of the coordinators listed in the chapter would be most helpful to your ministry?

Chapter 9: Beyond Rotation

1. What kind of response would you expect from your current volunteers if you asked them in February whether they planned to return in September?

2. Who are the people in your church who know people you don't know? Think of three or four people you could ask for referrals for your prospect list.

3. Can you think of a current volunteer who surprised you by saying yes? Who is it?

4. What will you have to change in your weekly routine to add focused, protected time for recruiting?

5. Is your volunteer rotation model working? If so, why is it working well? If not, what would you like to try after reading this chapter?

6. How can you make your next training event more attractive and meaningful for your volunteers?

Chapter 10: Beyond the Victim

1. Think of two or three people in your church you would like to call friends. How could you begin to cultivate those relationships?

2. What are some ways you can bring value to another ministry in the church?

3. What are some things you can do to elevate the profile of the children's ministry?

4. Who else serving in the children's ministry can you celebrate in a public way so others know what is happening in the ministry?

5. Name some of the people who need to know the vision and successes of the children's ministry.

Chapter 11: Children's Ministry Is Family Ministry

1. What are some events you could invite families in your community to in the coming year?

2. Who are some parents in your ministry that need to hear something good about their kids? What can you share with them?

3. Think of a successful event you're already doing that focuses on kids. How could you incorporate a parent component with that event?

4. Name two or three families you want to reach out to in the next week.

Chapter 12: More Than Planning

1. What do you look forward to planning in your first balcony-time session?

2. What will you need to change so you can take that balcony time?

3. How do you handle Sunday morning monkey management? What is one thing you'd like to change about that process?

4. Choose three things from this chapter to add to your own organizational system in the next month.

Chapter 13: Your Ministry Marathon

1. Do you have life-giving relationships outside of your church? If not, think of some friends that you need to reconnect with.

2. What do your friends and family think about the time you spend at church?

3. If you don't have a fun hobby, what is something you have always wanted to try?

4. When you feel yourself slipping into a negative state, what are some things that can bring you back?

5. Who has been a great coach for you in your ministry? If you don't have someone now, who would you like to have as a coach?

Chapter 14: Finding Your Bounce

1. Think of a time when you planned something that felt like a failure. How did you respond? What can you learn from that experience?

2. Who in your life gives you a great example of living with resilience?

3. How can you expand your constellation of coaches? Who would you like to add to your constellation and why?

4. What one thing can you change that will help you move from a ministry leader to a leader of leaders?

Notes

Introduction

5 *Give me a place*: This variant derives from an earlier source than Pappus: "Fragments of Book XXVI," *Diodorus Siculus: Library of History* 11, trans. F. R. Walton (Cambridge, MA: Harvard University Press, 1957).

3 Beyond Goldfish and Bubble Machines

30 This chapter is adapted from Annette Safstrom, "Content vs. Systems," Ministry Architects blog, March 24, 2015. Used with permission.

32-33 *Years of preparation*: Mark DeVries, *Sustainable Youth Ministry* (Downers Grove, IL: InterVarsity Press, 2008), 51-52.

7 Seeing What Others Can't—Yet

90 *begin with the end in mind*: Stephen Covey, *Seven Habits of Highly Effective People* (New York: Simon & Schuster, 1989), 14.

10 Beyond the Victim

131 *to deal with people*: "Politics," *Dictionary.com*, accessed June 5, 2017, www.dictionary.com/browse/politics?s+t.

132 *It's rarely malice*: Dan Reiland, "Church Politics: Part 1," Pneuma Foundation, accessed June 6, 2017, www.pneumafoundation.org /article.jsp?article=/article_0082.xml.

135 *malignant narcissism*: Scott Peck, *The People of the Lie*, 2nd ed. (New York: Touchstone, 1998), 78.

11 Children's Ministry Is Family Ministry

148 *For example, if you are sending*: TED is a nonprofit devoted to spreading ideas, usually in the form of short, powerful talks (18 minutes or less). See www.ted.com/talks.

12 More Than Planning

167 *In 1918, Charles Schwab*: James Clear, "The Ivy Lee Method: The Daily Routine Experts Recommend for Productivity," JamesClear .com, accessed June 6, 2017, http://jamesclear.com/ivy-lee.

13 Your Ministry Marathon

184 *A study at*: Mary P. Bennett, Janice M. Zeller, Lisa Rosenberg, and Judith McCann, "The Effect of Mirthful Laughter on Stress and Natural Killer Cell Activity," PubMed.gov, March-April 2003, www.ncbi.nlm .nih.gov/pubmed/12652882; Bill Seiler, "School of Medicine Study Shows Laughter Helps Blood Vessels Function Better," University of Maryland Medical Center, March 7, 2005, http://umm.edu/news -and-events/news-releases/2005/school-of-medicine-study-shows -laughter-helps-blood-vessels-function-better.

185 *The word* busy: Eugene H. Peterson, "The Unbusy Pastor," *Christianity Today*, 1981, www.christianitytoday.com/pastors/1981/summer /8113070.html.

Appendix G

222 This appendix was originally published in Mark DeVries *Sustainable Youth Ministry* (Downers Grove, IL: InterVarsity Press, 2008), 211-13. Used with permission.

Helping Churches Create Sustainable Change

There tends to be two very different types of people in ministry. The first focuses on systems, structures, and stability. The end result of their work is stability. The second is a disruptive innovator, one who brings energy, creativity, and a whirlwind of passion to a ministry.

Stability can quickly turn into sterility, and energetic change initiatives are often short-lived, personality-driven, and have a tendency to leave a path of disruption and instability in their wake.

There is a better way. The church needs both:

○ healthy systems

○ inspiring, catalytic innovation

The church needs sustainable change; change that sticks.

At Ministry Architects, we help churches navigate the challenging journey through change. We help you build the systems that ensure stability without sacrificing creativity and innovation. Change that lasts.

We are a team of experienced pastors, children's ministers, youth workers, and professors who provide coaching for ministry professionals and consult with churches and ministry teams to create sustainable change.

To find out how we can help you lead sustainable change in your church or ministry, contact us at

info@ministryarchitects.com

877-462-5718

This book also entitles you to take our Children's Ministry Diagnostic absolutely free. You can do so at

diagnostics.ministryarchitects.com

use the passcode SCMye4hu

More Titles from
InterVarsity Press

**Building Your
Volunteer Team**
978-0-8308-4121-9

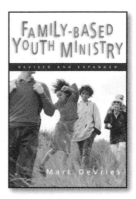

**Family-Based
Youth Ministry**
978-0-8308-3243-9

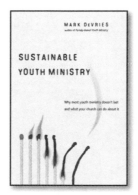

**Sustainable
Youth Ministry**
978-0-8308-3361-0

Please visit us at ivpress.com.

PRAXIS
EQUIPPING LEADERS FOR MINISTRY

"...TO EQUIP HIS PEOPLE FOR WORKS OF SERVICE,

SO THAT THE BODY OF CHRIST MAY BE BUILT UP."

EPHESIANS 4:12

God has called us to ministry. But it's not enough to have a vision for ministry if you don't have the practical skills for it. Nor is it enough to do the work of ministry if what you do is headed in the wrong direction. We need both vision *and* expertise for effective ministry. We need *praxis*.

Praxis puts theory into practice. It brings cutting-edge ministry expertise from visionary practitioners. You'll find sound biblical and theological foundations for ministry in the real world, with concrete examples for effective action and pastoral ministry. Praxis books are more than the "how to"—they're also the "why to." And because *being* is every bit as important as *doing*, Praxis attends to the inner life of the leader as well as the outer work of ministry. Feed your soul, and feed your ministry.

If you are called to ministry, you know you can't do it on your own. Let Praxis provide the companions you need to equip God's people for life in the kingdom.

www.ivpress.com/praxis